The FOA Reference Guide To Premises Cabling

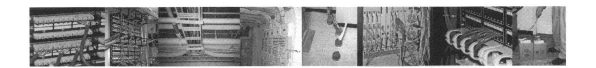

And Study Guide To FOA Certification

Jim Hayes

The Fiber Optic Association, Inc.
The Professional Society Of Fiber Optics
www.TheFOA.org

The FOA Reference Guide To Premises Cabling And Study Guide To FOA Certification

The Fiber Optic Association, Inc.

1119 S. Mission Road #355, Fallbrook, CA 92028
Telephone: 1-760-451-3655 Fax 1-781-207-2421
Email: info@thefoa.org   http://www.TheFOA.org

Updated February 2014.
Copyright 2010, 2014 The Fiber Optic Association, Inc.

CFOT© is a registered trademark of The Fiber Optic Association, Inc., US Patent and Trademark Office Reg. No. 3,572,190.

ISBN 1450559662

Table of Contents

Preface

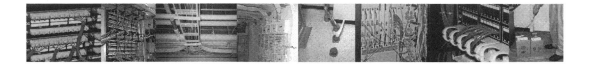

The Fiber Optic Association, Inc., the nonprofit professional society of fiber optics, has become one of the principal sources of technical information, training curriculum and certifications for the cabling industry. As technology has driven the rate of technical change ever faster, it has become a challenge to provide printed reference books that are not hopelessly out of date. Instead, many readers turn to the Internet for more up-to-date technical information.

The information on the Internet, however, is often biased, even that on supposedly non-commercial websites, and anonymous sources must be assumed to be untrustworthy or have a commercial agenda.

How, one might ask, can a "Fiber Optic Association" produce an unbiased book on premises cabling when so much of that cabling is copper and many users are migrating to wireless? Most cabling networks already depend on fiber optics for high speed backbones and new fiber optic cabling systems for premises applications based on FTTH architectures are being introduced. The FOA is focused on education, not selling products, and we think it's important that every tech knows as much as possible about copper, fiber and wireless technology so they can deal successfully with all three of them in premises cabling.

You will note that this book includes some topics not generally covered in cabling books, like coax and wireless, and ignores others like legacy POTS (plain old telephone service) lines because of their relative (lack of) importance in today's world. We also do not obsess over standards, covering them only to ensure the technician knows their proper use. With this new 2014 edition, we have added an appendix on optical LANs (OLANs) which are gaining acceptance in the market, but we feel are worth a special section separate from the current fiber optic chapter.

The FOA created its Online Reference Guide (www.foaguide.org) to provide a more up-to-date and unbiased reference for those seeking information on cabling and fiber optic technology, components, applications and installation. Its success confirms the assumption that most users prefer the Internet for technical information. For those interested in premises cabling, copper, fiber or connections to wireless access points, the Premises Cabling Systems section of the online reference guide provides a wealth of usable information. With this book, we address the needs for those who prefer printed books or who must have them to meet academic requirements. However, the production of this book is done by "publishing on demand," where the book is not printed until ordered, and only after accessing the latest version electronically. Thus this edition meets the needs of those who prefer printed references without burdening them with trying to determine what material is already obsolete.

For those who want this printed version but also want access to the web for color graphics, automatic self-testing or links to even more technical information, we suggest going to the FOA Online Reference Guide website to the appropriate sections covered in this book.

If you have feedback on the book, feel free to email comments or questions to the FOA at info@thefoa.org.

A note of appreciation

The material has been produced and reviewed by a number of contributors whom we wish to thank for their work in contributing, creating and reviewing the materials included here: Jim Hayes, Editor, Michael Hayes, editing and design, Reviewers: Bob Ballard, Duane Clayton, Tom Collins, Gary Giguere, Bill Graham, Karen Hayes, Ron Leger, Jim Underwood and many, many more.

This information is provided by The Fiber Optic Association, Inc. as a benefit to those interested in designing, manufacturing, selling, installing or using fiber optic communications, premises cabling systems or networks. It is intended to be used as a overview and/or basic guidelines and in no way should be considered to be complete or comprehensive. These guidelines are strictly the opinion of the FOA and the reader is expected to use them as a basis for learning, reference and creating their own documentation, project specifications, etc. Those working with fiber optics in the classroom, laboratory or field should follow all safety rules carefully. The FOA assumes no liability for the use of any of this material.

Chapter 1
Overview of Cabling

Objectives: From this chapter you should learn:
How communications and cabling developed
The role of cabling in communications
How standards develop and are used for interoperability
Differences between standards and codes

A Short History of Communications

The history of modern telecommunications spans slightly more than 150
years, starting with the development of the telegraph in the early 19th
century. Telegraphy gave man the means to transmit a series of impulses
that represented letters. When these letters were received and decoded, they
provided a way to convey messages over long distances.
Naturally, the next step was to consider whether sound might also somehow
be electrically transmitted. Alexander Graham Bell applied for his patent for
an "electrical speaking telephone" in 1876, beating Elisha Gray by only a
few hours. In reality, many people contributed to telephone improvements
including Thomas Alva Edison, Lars Ericsson and David Edward Hughes
whose invention of the microphone became universally used in telephones.
It is amazing how quickly the use of the telephone spread. The first
switchboard, an experiment, was installed in Boston in 1877. Just four years
later, there were 54,000 telephones in the United States! The first connections
from Boston to New York began in 1884. Wireless communications developed
from the work of Nikola Tesla and Guglielmo Marconi. In the first decade of
the 20th century, Dr. Lee deForest's invention of the vacuum tube amplifier
and telephone repeaters enabled long distance communications. So for the
first half of the twentieth century, communications spread worldwide using the
same basic technologies.
By the 1970s, integrated circuit technology and the microprocessor began to
influence telecommunications and computers. Experiments began in digital
voice transmission and fiber optics. Computer networks like Ethernet and the
predecessor of the Internet were developed.
The 1980s brought wide scale use of digital telecom, computer networks and
fiber optic long distance networks. The 1980s also brought the breakup of
the Bell system in the US and the spread of minicomputer and PC networks.

Users who once depended on AT&T for telecom standards and IBM or other computer companies for computing standards were left stranded. Manufacturers took up standards development to insure interoperability of their products under the auspices of the IEEE for computer networking electronics, EIA/TIA for cabling in the US and ISO and IEC worldwide. Thus was born the industry standards that we all depend on for today's communications networks.

Today everybody is connected via the Internet, more devices connect over wireless than cable and the fiber optic backbone that makes it all possible is being extended to directly connect homes. This fiber to the home technology is even being used in premises LANs to replace traditional structured cabling LANs which were based on earlier telephone technology, something which will be discussed later in the book.

But all telecommunications and the Internet depend on cabling. Typically, communications work on a worldwide fiber optic backbone connected into private networks that utilize a combination of copper, fiber and wireless connections.

What is Premises Cabling?

By premises cabling, we mean the cabling used inside buildings and in restricted geographic areas like campuses or among clustered business facilities that follows industry standards. Mostly we are referring to structured cabling systems defined by industry standards that are used for LANs, telephone systems and even other indoor or campus systems adapted to structured cabling like CCTV, security or building management.

Other Uses For Standardized Premises Cabling

TIA-568 originally considered the use of structured cabling to be corporate LANs, primarily Ethernet but some legacy IBM Token Ring. However the large-scale adoption of UTP cabling standards has gained the attention of many other applications. UTP is now used for CCTV cameras, security systems, building management systems, etc. Some of these systems have been redesigned for UTP cable while others require adapters, such as baluns, which convert coax to balanced UTP transmission. One can also get adapters that allow multiple equipment to use separate pairs of the UTP cable, for example: a POTS phone line and a Fast Ethernet connection. Most of these applications will also use fiber optics where the length or bandwidth exceeds the limitations of UTP copper cable.

What Are Cabling Standards?

Widespread usage of any technology depends on the existence of acceptable standards for components and systems. These standards are written as minimum specifications for components and systems that will ensure interoperability of equipment from various manufacturers.

During the 1980s, telecommunications and computer technology changed rapidly. Phone signals became digital, fiber proliferated. Minicomputers and personal computers became connected over local area networks (LANs). To support this rapid expansion of digital communications, new cables and cabling architecture were needed.

The goal was to make buildings "smart": able to allow computer and phone conversations over a standardized wiring system. By the early 1990s, a scheme of "structured cabling" was standardized by technical committee of a trade association: the merged Electronic Industries Association and Telecommunications Industry Association (hereafter referred to as EIA/TIA) in the USA and ISO/IEC worldwide.

This cabling standard, developed by what was then called the EIA/TIA TR 41.8 committee - now renamed TR 42 - is referred to by the number of the primary standard, EIA/TIA 568, although there are actually a number of standards, technical advisories, etc. that cover all aspects of structured cabling. Most people simply say "568" when they mean the entire output of the TR 42 committee which includes a number of standards described below. TIA-568 is a US standard. Overseas, ISO/IEC controls similar standards and a summary of their standards is below. There is a movement to rationalize international standards which has led to dropping of some TIA standards in lieu of ISO/IEC standards.

The model for premises cabling standards was AT&T's design guidelines for communications cabling developed originally from a 1982 survey of 79 businesses located in New York, California, Florida and Arkansas involving over 10,000 cable runs. At the time, cabling was used mainly for telephones to wiring closets and PBXes (Private Branch Exchanges or local phone switches), but it established a baseline for cable length requirements for commercial customers that was used in creating TIA-568. The AT&T survey determined that 99.9% of all stations were less than 300 feet (about 100 meters) from the wiring closet, so that became the goal of the TIA 568 standard. Much of the terminology from the telephone industry also carried over into the development of structured cabling standards, although some of that terminology is being replaced by less telephone-specific terminology.

Today's cabling standards define cabling systems, using both copper and fiber optic cables that can support premises networks called LANs for "local area networks" from 10 megabits per second to 10 gigabits per second over 100 meter distances.

Cabling standards are not developed for end users or installers, but for component and equipment manufacturers. The manufacturers develop products around the standards specifications and are responsible for telling

installers and end users how to use these components. The designers, installers and users of networks can rely on the instructions of the manufacturers on how to utilize these "standard products" correctly.
The essence of standards for structured cabling is they provide a minimum performance level for components and cabling systems that manufacturers use to develop products for the marketplace. The competition in the cabling marketplace requires companies to make cables that are better than those standards in order to differentiate their products from competitors. So using those standards, manufacturers make cables that will be compatible with other cables meeting the same standards but offer advantages in performance, installation or cost.

Codes or Standards?

Many people think this standard is a mandatory, even legal, document like the US National Electric Code (see below.) In fact, 568 is *a voluntary interoperability standard* for communications cabling, developed by a number of manufacturers of cabling components and networking equipment. This enables manufacturers to make compatible cabling components and equipment that could be used with any standards-compliant cabling system and allow upgrading in the future as long as the equipment was designed for the same standardized cable plant.
What 568 is, in fact, is a common sense approach to cabling that defines component and cabling system specifications and offers interoperability, upgradeability and low cost due to the numerous manufacturers offering compatible products.
Codes refer to legal requirements for cabling and networks that are generally adopted to ensure safe working environments. Codes cover flammability for fire safety and various electrical safety issues including parallel routing of cables, grounding and bonding. Codes may differ in various locations due to the local laws. When in doubt, contact local building and electrical inspectors to determine requirements.

The Basics of the "568" Standards

The TIA "568" cabling standard calls for connecting the desktop (work area) to a telecom closet (the "horizontal" run) with up to 100 meters of cable (including 90 m of permanently installed cable (permanent link) and no more than 10 m total of patchcords), which is usually unshielded twisted pair - UTP - with 4 pairs of wires - called Cat 3, Cat 5, Cat5e, Cat 6 or Cat 6A. The "Cat" or "category" designation refers to a performance level or grade, which we will explain in the Cables section. Most copper installations today use Cat 5e or Cat 6 exclusively, as they aren't that much more expensive than Cat 3 and can support phones or any LAN on any outlet. Screened twisted pair (foil shielded over the 4 pairs) and shielded twisted pair (STP) are also acceptable.

The backbone cabling can be either UTP or fiber optics. In larger networks, fiber is most often used for its longer distance capability and higher bandwidth. 568 specifies two multimode fibers, 62.5/125, the most common MM fiber until recently, and 50/125, a higher bandwidth fiber rated for use with lasers for gigabit networks that is rapidly overtaking 62.5/125 in popularity. Singlemode fiber is also specified for longer backbone links for high speed networks; for example: a campus network.

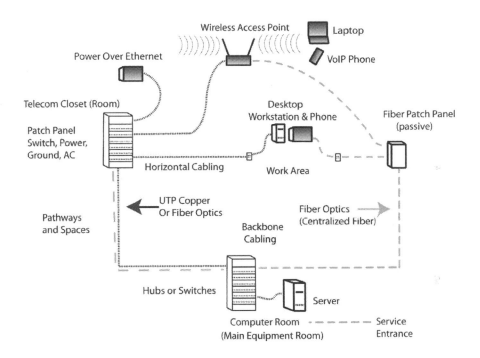

Fiber optics is also a horizontal option in 568, but not often used because of the higher cost except where high bit-rate networks or future upgrades are expected. However, a properly designed centralized fiber network that connects the desktop directly to the computer room with no intermediate electronics does not need a telecom closet and saves the cost of conditioned power, data ground, AC and the floor space, which may offset the additional cost of the fiber electronics.

Virtually every corporate network now includes wireless, which is, of course, not wireless - access points are connected into the network with copper or fiber cabling.

The telecom closet, or telecom room (TR), as it is now called, houses the hubs for the computers in the work areas. These hubs are interconnected on "backbone" wiring which is mostly fiber optics, as it usually carries higher speed signals over longer distances and provides isolation from ground loops, another problem with copper cabling in LANs. The main cross-connect (MXC) or equipment room contains the network and telco hardware. Telephones (whose lower bandwidth requirements allow longer runs) are usually simply connected to backbone cables in the telecom closet with a punchdown and run straight to the MXC.

TIA 568 standards have also included IBM Type 1 cable, a shielded two pair cable, since it is still used in some networks. However, it does not include coax cable, like RG-58 used in some Ethernet LANs and RG-6 used in CATV and CCTV, except in the residential standard.

The TIA-568-C and D revision propose to change the nomenclature of structured cabling systems. A review of this proposed change is in Appendix D.

Cabling Standards Beyond "568"

568 is only part of the structured cabling standards. It's a multi-part standard itself and there are several more standards cover other areas of cabling:
EIA/TIA 568: The main standard document for structured cabling, usually referred to as simply "568." It is now on the "C" revision, published in 2009. *Always check with manufacturers for the latest revisions.*

EIA/TIA 569: Covers pathways and spaces. Defines the "telecom closet" or telecom room as it is now called.
EIA/TIA 570: Residential cabling.
EIA/TIA 606: Cabling system administration (documentation).
EIA/TIA 607: Grounding and bonding.

International Standards

The international equivalent of EIA/TIA 568 is ISO/IEC 11801. The standards are written similarly to what has been done by TR 42. Here are their relevant standards:

ISO/IEC 11801: Cabling for customer premises - structured cabling similar to TIA 568.
ISO/IEC 14763-1: Administration, documentation - similar to TIA 606.
ISO/IEC 14763-2: Planning and Installation - similar to TIA 569.
ISO/IEC 14763-3: Testing optical fibre cabling - included in TIA 568.
IEC 61935-1: Testing copper cabling - included in TIA 568.

Electrical Codes For Cabling

The most important "standards" and the only ones that are legally mandatory are the local building and electrical codes, such as the US National Electrical Code (NEC.) The NEC is developed by the National Fire Protection Assn. and covers all aspects of electrical and fire safety. Article 800 of the NEC covers communication circuits, such as telephone systems and outside wiring for fire and burglar alarm systems and Article 770 covers fiber optics. All premises cabling must comply with building and electrical codes applicable in your area. Below is a listing of current NEC articles covering premises cabling.

NEC Articles Covering Cabling

Chapter	Article	Topic
2	250	Grounding and Bonding
6	640	Sound Systems
7	725	Remote-Control, Signaling and Power-Limited Circuits
7	760	Fire Alarm Signaling Systems
7	770	Optical Fiber Cables and Raceways
7	780	"Smart House" Wiring
8	800	Telecommunications Circuits (Telephone and LAN)
8	810	Radio and TV Equipment
8	820	CATV Systems
8	830	Network-Powered Broadband Systems

Learning More About Standards and Codes

There are a number of ways of finding out more about cabling standards and codes, but first you need to decide what you need to know. Cabling standards were written by manufacturers to have standard product specifications they could use for developing products that would work together. Network developers have a standardized cable plant for which they develop networks. Users know that standard communications networks will work on standard cabling systems.

Thus manufacturers of cabling components need to know all the details in the standards to ensure their products meet those standards. Network designers only need to know the performance specifications of the standardized cabling so they can design networks that operate over cabling that meet those standards. End users basically need to specify that cabling meets the standards. Contractors and installers need to know what products meet those standards and how to install them, information they should get from the manufacturers of cabling products, not the standards themselves.

So basically, only manufacturers of cabling products really need the actual standards documents. Others can rely on the manufacturers to provide the performance, design and installation information they need. You can get catalogs and/or visit the websites of a number of cabling manufacturers who have extremely complete explanations of the standards which have been created for their installers and end users.

Codes are more important since they are legal requirements and will be the regulations used for inspection of installations. Understanding codes requires not only learning what codes cover but what codes are applicable in the local area and who inspects installations. Furthermore, codes change regularly, usually every 2-5 years, and installers are required to keep up to date on the codes. Understand what is required in the areas you do installations and know when the codes are updated. Also be aware than many states or cities require licensing of cabling installers just like electricians, so it is important to know the local requirements.

The "Cables" of "Cabling"

The choice of cable in network cabling (or communication medium as it is sometimes called) is rather important because of the extremely high frequencies of the signals. Sending a 60-cycle utility power through a wire rarely presents a difficulty; but sending a 1 or 10 billion bits per second signal can be a lot more difficult. For this reason, the method of sending signals and the materials they are sent through can be important.

Network Cabling Types

A number of cabling options have been developed over the history of communications and are still in use for networking connections.

Unshielded Twisted pair (UTP) - UTP cable is the primary cable used for networks, as specified in the EIA/TIA 568 standard. UTP was developed from the original phone wires but refined to enhance its bandwidth capability. This cable type has been widely used because it is inexpensive and simple to install. The limited bandwidth of early UTP (which translates into slower transmissions) has pushed development of new cable performance grades (the "categories" of 568) but has created a more expensive product and more complicated installation process.

Screened Twisted pair (ScTP) - Same as UTP with an overall shield around the 4 pairs. While not currently specified for any networks or covered in the EIA/TIA 568 standard (but not prohibited), it is used in many networks in Europe where EMI is a greater concern. It tends to be more expensive, harder to terminate and requires special shielded plugs and jacks.

Shielded Twisted Pair (STP) - Like UTP but with a shield around every pair. It is widely used in IBM systems (IBM Type 1 cable) and included in early versions of 568.

Coaxial Cables - The original Ethernet cable was coax and coax is still used in video (CCTV, CATV) systems. This is familiar and easy to install, has good bandwidth and lower attenuation but more expensive and bulky. It is not included in 568, but in 570, for residential video use. Coax is also used in residential applications for LANs using a transmission scheme called MoCA that works like a cable modem.

Optical Fiber - Optional for most networks, it has top performance, excellent bandwidth, very long life span, and excellent security but slightly higher installed cost than twisted pair cables. Fiber requires additional electronics to interface to them. Fiber can be cost effective with optimal architecture, such as centralized fiber or passive optical LANs.

Other transmission options:

Wireless - No data transmission cables are required to connect any individual terminal, but wireless requires cabling to every antenna (called an Access Point.) A terminal can be moved anywhere within the range of the radio signals. Usually wireless is more expensive but can be used in locations where it would be difficult to install cables. In the modern network, wireless is a requirement because so many users want "mobility" - so they are not "tethered" to a desktop.

Infrared Transmission - Also transmits data without wires or fibers using infrared (IR) light but each transmitter requires cabling. By sending pulses of infrared light in the same patterns as electronic pulses sent over cables, it is possible to send data from one place to another. Networks based on IR transmission have been developed for use in office and for line-of-sight transmissions between buildings. It is generally limited in range and can be interrupted by blocking or weather.

Powerline or Phone Line Transmission - Networks using available power line cabling have been under development for many years, but with mixed results due the unpredictability of wiring performance and interference from power line noise.

We will focus only on the most popular types of cabling, UTP, coax and fiber optics, as well as cabling for wireless.

Further Study
Review the premises cabling topics on the FOA Online Reference Guide

at www.foaguide.org

Review Questions

Multiple Choice
Identify the choice that best completes the statement or answers the question.

_____1.   What is the standard everyone in the USA refers to as the basis
of structured cabling?
A. IEEE 802.3
B. EIA/TIA 568
C. EIA/TIA TR42
D. NEMA 63.1999

_____2.   What is the international standard for structured cabling?
A. TIA-568
B. ISO-11801
C. ISO-9000
D. IEC-0001

_____3.   What copper cable types are included in the TIA-568
structuredcabling standards?
A. UTP (unshielded twisted pair), STP (shielded twisted pair)
and coax
B. UTP (unshielded twisted pair) and coax
C. UTP (unshielded twisted pair), ScTP (screened twisted pair)
and STP (shielded twisted pair)
D. Any communications cable

_____4.   What do Category 3, Category 5e and Category 6 designations
mean?
A. How well the cables are made
B. Flame retardance of the cable
C. How far the cable will work in networks
D. The performance level of UTP cable

_____5.   What is the cable from the telecom closet (room) to the work area
called?
A. Horizontal cabling

    B. Backbone cabling
    C. Work area cable
    D. Patchcord

_____6.   What is the cabling from the telecom closet to the main cross connect or computer center called?
    A. Horizontal cabling
    B. Backbone cabling
    C. Riser cable
    D. Patchcord

_____7.   Why is the structured cabling standard not like "code"?
    A. It doesn't deal with flammability
    B. It is not legally required
    C. It changes every year
    D. It is not written by the NFPA

_____8.   What other cables are recognized in the structured cabling standards?
    A. CATV RG-6 coax
    B. IBM Type II
    C. Multimode fiber optic cable
    D. Singlemode and multimode fiber optic cable

_____9.   What is the maximum length of a permanently installed UTP cabling link allowed in structured cabling standards?
    A. 90 meters
    B. 100 meters
    C. 100 feet
    D. Depends on the electronics running on the link

Matching

Structured cabling architecture: Match the letter in the drawing with the definition below.

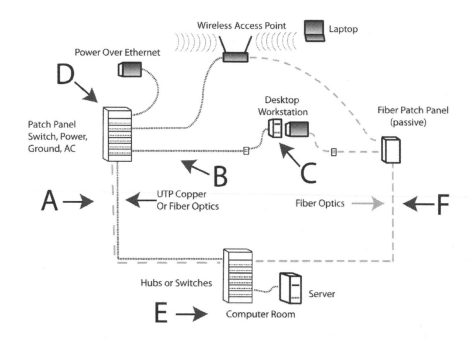

_____10.   Main cross connect

_____11.   Telecom closet (room)

_____12.   Backbone cabling

_____13.   Horizontal cabling

_____14.   Centralized fiber cabling

_____15.   Work area

Additional Study and Projects

Review manufacturers' literature on TIA structured cabling standards. The manufacturers build products to TIA standards but are responsible for interpreting them for their customers. Most manufacturers have sections on the standards in their catalogs and on their websites.

The NFPA which writes the US National Electrical Code publishes a book called "Limited Energy Systems" that details how premises cabling systems are covered in the NEC. This book is an excellent reference for contractors and installers.

Chapter 2
Cabling Jargon

Objectives: From this chapter you should learn:
The language of premises cabling
Meaning of specialized cabling terms

The key to understanding any technology is understanding the language
of the technology – the jargon. We've started this book with an overview of
cabling jargon to introduce you to the language of premises cabling and to
help you understand what you will be reading in the book. We suggest you
read this section first to help your understanding of the rest of the book and
refer back to it when you encounter a term that you do not recognize.

What is Premises Cabling?

By premises cabling, we mean the cabling used inside buildings (and in
restricted geographic areas like campuses or among business facilities)
that follow industry standards. Mostly we are referring to structured cabling
systems defined by TIA-568 or ISO/IEC 11801 and related standards that
are used for LANs, telephone systems and even other systems adapted
to structured cabling like CCTV, security or building management. Other
systems that depend on cabling such as security and building control
are migrating to structured cabling for its widespread availability and
predictability.

Here's an overview of the basic jargon used in cabling:

To begin with, what do we call this technology of cabling?
People call it lots of things:
VDV (for voice/data/video) cabling
Premises (e.g. indoor) cabling
Structured cabling (from the standards)
Data/voice cabling
Low voltage cabling (less than power cables)
Limited energy cabling (mostly harmless)
Teledata cabling (a made-up word from telecommunications and data)

Datacom cabling (an abbreviated version of data communications)

Most people call it "premises cabling" for its application or "structured cabling" after the "568" standard.

Premises cabling is the infrastructure for telephone and LAN connections in most commercial installations and even in some modern homes. It's also used for fire alarms, building management, audio and video.

Structured cabling is the standardized architecture and components for communications cabling specified by the EIA/TIA TR42 committee and used as a voluntary standard by manufacturers to insure interoperability.

Cabling Standards

Structured cabling is based on a number of industry standards - voluntary interoperability standards - developed by manufacturers who want their products to work together. They meet in committees several times a year and decide on the specifications of their products. These common specs mean that equipment will work on any cabling system that follows the standards and most cabling components can be interchanged without adversely affecting performance.

EIA/TIA: In the US, Electronics Industry Alliance/Telecommunications Industry Association (TIA), is an industry trade association that creates voluntary interoperability standards for the products made by member companies. Worldwide standards rely on ISO and IEC standards.

EIA/TIA 568: The main standard document for structured cabling, usually referred to as simply "568." It is now on the "C" revision, published in 2009. Worldwide, ISO/IEC 11801 is approximately the same as TIA-568.

EIA/TIA 569: Covers pathways and spaces. Defines the "telecom closet" or telecom room as it is now called (ISO/IEC 14763-2).

EIA/TIA 570: For residential cabling.

EIA/TIA 606: Cabling system administration (documentation) (ISO/IEC 14763-1).

EIA/TIA 607: Grounding and bonding.

Standards are not code! They are voluntary interoperability specifications. However, every installation must be compliant to local building codes for safety!

NEC (National Electrical Code): Written by NFPA (National Fire Protection Assn). This code sets standards for fire protection for construction and is a legal requirement in most cities.

Structured Cabling Architecture

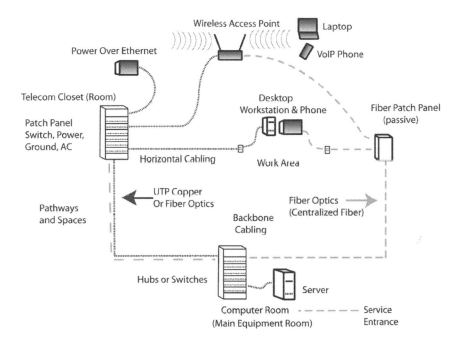

LANs are now being built using the architecture and equipment of fiber to the home (FTTH) networks. See appendix B for details.

Structured Cabling Terms

The terms listed here are the traditional terms used since the beginning of structured cabling, but a new set of terminology is being introduced (see Appendix B).

Telecom Closet (TC): The location of the connection between horizontal cabling to the backbone. Now often called "Telecom Room" to imply it's usually bigger than a closet!

Main Cross-Connect (MXC): The old telco term for the location of the main electronics in a building. LAN people may call it the equipment room.

Intermediate Cross-Connect (IXC): A room in between the TC and MXC where cables are terminated.
(TIA has proposed to change these terms in future standards. See Appendix B.)

Work Area Outlet: The jack on the wall which is connected to the desktop computer by a patchcord.

Patch Panel: A rack or box where cables are terminated - usually in 110 punchdowns and interconnected with patchcords.

Horizontal Cabling: The connection from the telecom closet to the work area outlet (desktop).

Backbone Cabling: The cabling that connects all the hubs in telecom closets or MXCs together.

Link (Permanent Link): The installed cable plant from work area outlet jack to the patch panel in the telecom closet.

Channel: The cable plant including the link plus patchcords on either end to connect the communications hardware.

Patchcord: A short length of stranded cable with a RJ-45 plug on either end, used to connect hardware to the link or to connect cables in a Patch Panel. Also a short fiber optic cable use for connections.

J hook: A hook shaped like the letter J used to suspend cables.

Fishtape: Semi-flexible rod used to retrieve cables or pull line.

Cable

The Types Of "Low Voltage" Copper Cable:
For information on fiber optic cabling, *see the FOA Online Fiber Optic Reference Guide.*

UTP: Unshielded twisted pair cable, most commonly comprised of 4 twisted pairs of copper conductors, graded for bandwidth as "Levels" (from Anixter) or "Categories" (EIA/TIA 568). Legacy analog phone systems (POTS or plain old telephone systems) used multipair UTP cables with 25, 50, 100, 200 or more pairs.

Category 3,4,5, 5e, 6, 6A: Ratings on the bandwidth performance of UTP cable, derived from Anixter's Levels program. Category 5e (enhanced) is rated to 100MHz. Cat 6 standards for UTP are specified at up to 200 MHz. Cat 6A (augmented) up to 500 MHz has recently been ratified. Cat 7 is also discussed for the future, but is only standardized as "Class F" in Europe, not the US. "Categories", called "Classes" in worldwide standards, like ISO and

IEC. Cables rated Cat 5 or higher are limited to 4 pairs.

A typical Cat 6 cable is shown below.

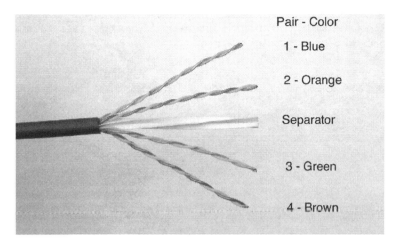

Pair - Color

1 - Blue

2 - Orange

Separator

3 - Green

4 - Brown

STP: Shielded twisted pair, specified by IBM for Token Ring networks and offered by some vendors in higher performance versions than UTP.

ScTP: Screened Twisted Pair, a UTP cable with an overall foil shield to prevent interference.

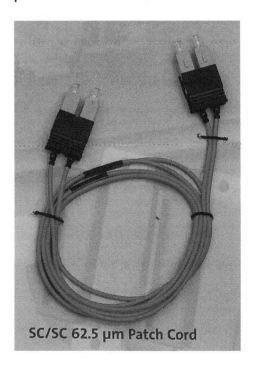

SC/SC 62.5 µm Patch Cord

Optical Fiber: Both multimode and singlemode fiber are included as well. *See the chapter on Fiber Optics, The Basics in the FOA Online Reference Guide or Lennie Lightwave's Guide to Fiber Optics for more information on fiber optics.*

Coax: A type of cable that uses a central conductor, insulation, outer conductor/shield, and jacket; used for high frequency communications like CCTV (closed circuit TV) or CATV (community antenna TV or cable TV). Coax is not included in TIA-568 but is included in TIA-570 for home use.

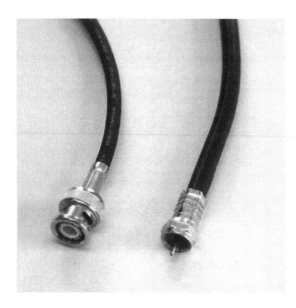

RG-6/RG-59: 75 ohm coax used for video. RG-6 is the standard for CATV, RG-59 is used on some short CCTV networks.

RG-58: 50 ohm coax used for "Thinnet" Ethernet.

HFC: Hybrid fiber-coax CATV network combines coax and optical fiber.

Terminations

The connectors for UTP are also standard - used on every cable for Cat 3, 5, 5e, 6, but must be rated for the same performance level, e.g. Cat 6 hardware on Cat 6 cable.

RJ-45: The popular name of the modular 8 pin connector used with UTP cable in structured cabling systems. It is used erroneously, as a connector is only really an RJ-45 if it is terminated with USOC pinout for plain old telephone service.

Jack: The receptacle for a modular plug like the modular 8 pin connector, often used in large quantities in patch panels (left in the photo above).

Plug: The connector on the end of UTP cable (right in the photo above).

Punchdown: A connecting block that terminates two cables directly, most often used for connecting incoming multipair cables to 4 pair cables to the desktop but occasionally for cross connecting 4 pair cables. 110 blocks are most popular for LANs, 66 blocks for telco, but some installers use BIX or Krone.

Below - 66 blocks on the left, 110 blocks on the right:

Cable Testing

After installing cables, they must be tested. Every cable, including Cat 3 for telephones, must be tested for wiremap, but cable certifiers will test for all the parameters listed below.

Wiremap: All eight wires must be connected to the correct pins, and the test is called a wiremap test.

Length: The length must be less than 90 m for the permanent link and less than 100 m for the channel.

Attenuation: The reduction in signal strength due to loss in the cable.

NEXT (Near End Cross Talk): The signal coupled from one pair to another in UTP cable.

ACR (Attenuation to Crosstalk Ratio): A measure of how much more signal than noise exists in the link by comparing the attenuated signal from one pair at the receiver to the crosstalk induced in the same pair.

Return Loss: Reflection from an impedance mismatch in a copper cable.

ELFEXT (Equal Level Far End Crosstalk): Crosstalk at the far end with signals of equal level being transmitted.

Propagation Delay: The time it takes a signal to go down the cable.

DC Loop Resistance: The DC resistance of the cable in ohms.

Delay Skew: The maximum difference of propagation time in all pairs of a cable.

Power Sum Next: Near end crosstalk tested with all pairs but one energized to find the total amount of crosstalk caused by simultaneous use of all pairs for communication.

Power Sum ELFEXT: ELFEXT for the sum of the other 3 pairs on the 4th pair.

PSACR: PowerSum ACR.

Alien Crosstalk: Crosstalk from one pair in a cable to the equivalent pair in another cable, a problem with Cat 6A.

Fiber Testing: Testing optical fiber is much easier. One need only test the loss from one end to the other, as bandwidth or frequency response is not generally an issue for premises cabling.

Networks

The Electronics

Hub: The electronic box that connects to all the horizontal cables which are then connected by backbone cabling, enabling any PC to talk to any other.

Switch: A device like a hub but connects any two devices directly, allowing multiple connections simultaneously.

Bridge: A device that connects two or more sets of network cables.

Router: A smart switch that connects to the outside world.

Ethernet: A 10, 100 or 1000 Megabit per second local area network (LAN) that is by far the most popular LAN.

10Base-T (10 MB/s Base Band Transmission): 100 meters max, segment length on Cat 3, or better twisted pair cable.

100Base-TX (100 MB/s Base Band Transmission): 100 meters max, segment length on Cat 5, twisted-pair cable, also referred to as Fast Ethernet.

1000Base-T: Gigabit Ethernet on Cat 5e UTP.

10GBase-T: 10 Gigabit Ethernet on Cat 6A UTP.

All versions of Ethernet also have fiber optic connection standards.

Power over Ethernet: The IEEE 802.3 Ethernet committee added provisions for powering devices off the spare pairs in a 4-pair UTP cable. Since Ethernet, up to 100Base-TX, uses only pairs 2 and 3, pairs 1 and 4 are available to provide power. Pair 1 (pins 4/5) is the + conductor, pair 4 (pins 7/8) is the - conductor. Almost 13 watts of power are available in IEEE 802.3af, 25W in IEEE 802.3at, adequate for powering VoIP phones or many wireless access points, thus saving cabling costs.

Wireless Is NOT Wireless

Most LANs today include wireless access points. Wireless is by no means wireless as it requires wiring to connect it to the network. It merely replaces patchcords with a wireless link to allow roaming within a limited area. Wireless requires many access points connected (over wire or fiber) into the backbone.

WiFi: The popular name for IEEE 802.11 standard used by most portable computers and many other mobile devices.

Bluetooth (IEEE 802.15): A limited distance network for consumer devices. It has been used to connect a wireless printer or mouse to a PC, wireless headsets to cell phones and stereos, cell phones to cars for hands-free operation, digital cameras to printers, etc.

WiMAX (IEEE 802.16): A further development of wireless network technology that expands the data capacity of wireless and it's distance capability.

Test Equipment and Tools For Cabling

Digital Multimeter: A simple tester that measures if the cable is shorted and whether or not it is open.

Wire Mapper: Checks each wire to make sure they are terminated in the correct order.

Cable Certification Tester: Tests everything, wiremap, length, attenuation and crosstalk in one connection, and gives you a pass/fail result.

Cable Verification Tester: A device that runs network signals over installed cabling to see if the cabling can transmit network data without error.

TDR (Time Domain Reflectometer): A testing device used for copper cable that operates like radar to find length, shorts or opens, and impedance mismatches.

Fiber optics: Testing is done with visual tracers/fault locators, optical loss test sets and OTDRs.

Further Study
Review the premises cabling topics on the FOA Online Reference Guide at www.foaguide.org

Review Questions

True/False
Indicate whether the statement is true or false.

_____1.   Premises cabling refers to cabling used for communications inside a building or limited to a campus.

_____2.   Cabling standards are mandatory requirements for cables installed to meet building and electrical codes.

_____3.   UTP cable can be used to power many devices such as VoIP phones and low speed wireless access points.

_____4.   Fiber optic testing is easier than copper testing since only insertion loss needs testing for premises cabling.

Multiple Choice
Identify the choice that best completes the statement or answers the question.

_____5.   _____ is the standard which forms the basis of structured cabling in the US?
A. IEEE 802.3
B. EIA/TIA 568
C. EIA/TIA TR42
D. NEMA 63.1999

_____6.   The international standard for structured cabling is _____?
A. TIA-568
B. ISO-11801
C. ISO-9000
D. IEC-0001

_____7.   What cable types are included in the TIA-568 structured cabling standards?
A. UTP (unshielded twisted pair), STP (shielded twisted pair) and coax
B. UTP (unshielded twisted pair) and coax
C. UTP (unshielded twisted pair), ScTP (screened twisted pair) and STP (shielded twisted pair)
D. UTP (unshielded twisted pair), ScTP (screened twisted pair), STP (shielded twisted pair) and fiber optics

_____8.   What do category ratings of UTP cable (e.g. Cat 3, Cat 5e, Cat 6 and Cat 6A) mean?
A. How well the cables are made
B. Flame retardance of the cable
C. How far the cable will work in networks
D. The performance level of UTP cable

_____9.   What is the cable from the telecom room (closet) to the work area called?
A. Horizontal cabling
B. Backbone cabling
C. Work area cable
D. Patchcord

_____10.   What is the installed cable plant from the work area outlet jack to the patch panel in the telecom closet called?
A. Permanent link
B. Channel
C. Link cable
D. Patchcord

_____11.   Why is the structured cabling standard not like "code"?
A. It's voluntary, not required by law
B. It doesn't deal with flammability
C. It changes every year
D. It is not written by the NFPA

_____12.   A category-rated UTP cable (Cat 3/5e/6/6A) used for horizontal cabling has _____ color coded pairs of wires.
A. 2
B. 4
C. 25
D. Any even number

Additional Study and Projects
Review manufacturers' websites and catalogs to see what premises cabling products are available. See if they use the same terminology and how they explain the usage of their products.

Chapter 3
Communications Networks and Applications

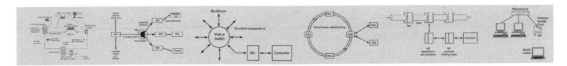

Objectives: From this chapter you should learn:
How computer networks use cabling for connections
Types of cabling used in networks
The use of unshielded twisted pair copper and optical fiber cabling
The choice among copper, fiber and wireless connections
Other applications of cabling

Computer Networks

Computer networks began long before PCs, going back to the 1960s when
mainframes were common and minicomputers were first introduced. The
goal of networking was, of course, sharing data among users. Then as now,
networking requires each user to have a unique "address," a protocol for
data to be formatted to make sharing easy and a means of transferring data.
Sharing data between computers and users over cables originally required
high speed cables, usually coax but also shielded twisted pair.

For many years, networks were mostly proprietary, that is they worked only
among computers made by one company such as IBM, Wang or DEC (Digital
Equipment Corp.). In the 1970s, multi-platform networks like ARCnet and
Ethernet were developed to allow different computer types to network and in
the 1980s, networking took off with the introduction of the inexpensive PC.

Computer Network Architectures

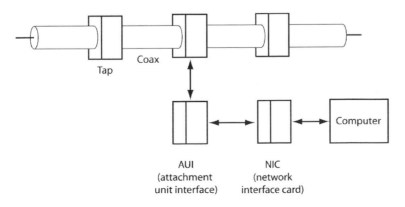

The first networks like Ethernet, Arcnet, WangNet and DecNet used coax cable for as a transmission medium because it offered the highest bandwidth. Coax was used as a data bus, with network attachments connected along the cable. Thus every network device received all data transmitted but ignored any that were not addressed to it.

Other networks, primarily IBM's Token Ring, used shielded twisted pair cable connected into a ring. In a ring, every network attachment is a repeater, receiving data from the network, filtering out messages for itself and passing others along. The same architecture was adopted for Fiber Distributed Data Interface (FDDI) which was the first all fiber high speed network. FDDI, shown here, used a dual ring architecture to allow the network to survive failure of either a cable segment or a network station. Some FDDI stations connected to the counter-rotating ring backbone (dual-attached stations (DAS) or dual-attached concentrators (DAC) which could also connect single-attached stations (SAS) onto one ring.

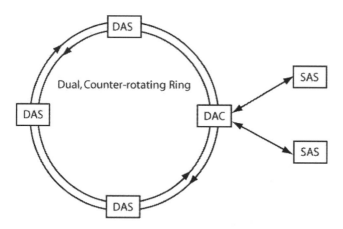

UTP (Unshielded Twisted Pair) cabling became a standard primarily to support the two most popular computer networks, Ethernet and IBM Token Ring. Although Ethernet was originally developed as a "bus" network using taps on coax cable and Token Ring used a "ring" architecture on shielded twisted pair cables, both were easily adapted to UTP cabling. The development of balanced transmission techniques for UTP cable provided a lower cost cabling alternative to both networks. Ethernet, because of its higher performance and lower cost became the preferred network for PCs and Token Ring fell into obsolescence.

As computer networking grew in popularity, new types of cables were developed to handle the multi-megabit data rates needed by computer networks. Fiber optics was used for the higher speed networks but at that time was much more expensive than copper cabling. A new method of using twisted pair cable, similar to phone wire but made to higher standards, was developed. Twisted pair cable was cheaper and easier to install so it be came the most popular cable type for computer networks very quickly.

The change from coax to UTP required a change in architecture for Ethernet. Ethernet originally used taps on the thick coax cable or a "T" in smaller RG-58 cable called ThinNet. UTP cable could only be used as a direct link from electronics to electronics, from the Network Interface Card (NIC) in a PC to a hub or switch that connects to the network backbone. When UTP was adopted, it required electronics to connect the links and create what is called a "star" network where PCs are connected to hubs or switches and hubs/switches are connected to the backbone. Even wireless antennas, called "access points," require cabling connections into the network.

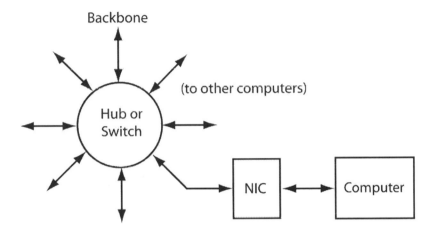

In order to convert the bus structure of Ethernet to UTP with a star architecture, an electronic repeater called a hub was used. Any signal transmitted into a hub would be repeated and sent to all equipment (either PCs or other hubs) attached to the hub. Each attached device was responsible for decoding addresses to pick up the messages being sent to it. Later, switches were adopted, since they directed messages only to the device being addressed, opening up additional bandwidth on the network.

With the acceptance of structured cabling, the cable plant architecture adopted the "star" architecture used in business phone systems along with many of the specifications and nomenclature developed primarily by AT&T before divestiture. Initially, copper cabling was used for both the backbone and horizontal connections. As networks became bigger and faster, backbone traffic increased to a point that most users migrated to optical fiber for the backbone to take advantage of its higher bandwidth. Large data users, like engineering and graphics, used fiber directly to the desktop using a centralized fiber architecture that has been adopted as a part of cabling standards. The diagram below illustrates how computer networks are connected over structured cabling.

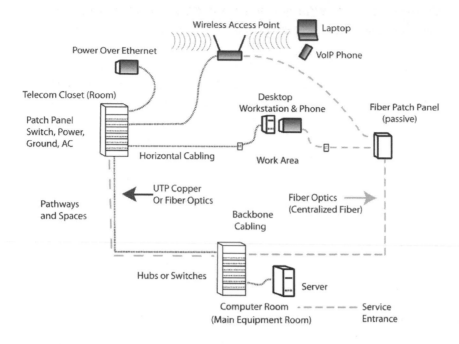

Residential, Industrial and Other Uses For Structured Cabling

While structured cabling is primarily thought of as cabling for enterprise computer networks, it is actually used from other purposes. Residential networks, security systems, industrial controls, building management systems and other systems developed for running on other cable types now offer UTP versions.

Many security systems now offer versions that can operate on standard structured cabling, not just for alarms or entry systems, but even for video. Most of these systems operated on some kind of twisted pair cable anyway, so converting to the standardized category-rated UTP was simple. Although video cameras generally run on coax, they can use UTP by converting the signals using a simple passive device called a balun or to fiber using an appropriate media converter.

Industrial applications of structured cabling are widespread. Most machines today are computer controlled and are connected to a network to receive programming instructions and upload manufacturing data. Industrial robots, especially, are controlled by network data and often even include plastic optical fibers inside the unit itself for control circuits because of fiber's flexibility and immunity to electrical noise.

Residential networks have grown rapidly as homes are connected to faster and faster internet connections to keep up with the growing numbers of PCs in the home and demands for more data over the Internet, digital video downloads and IPTV (Internet Protocol TV.) More homes are now connected with optical fiber or DSL over copper at multi-megabit speeds. Inside the home, most already have coax cables for TV, but some homes are now built with UTP cabling for digital networks. Wireless and MOCA, a network that connects PCs over the CATV coax, are also used.

TIA in the US has standards covering residential (TIA 570) and industrial (TIA 1005) structured cabling. TIA 570 allows the usual UTP versions plus video (CATV or Satellite TV) on coax. Although some consumer electronics use inexpensive plastic optical fiber (POF) for TOSLINK or FireWire (IEEE 1394) links, these are not considered part of TIA 570 because they are not permanently installed cabling but only local connections between devices.

Data Centers

Data centers are one of the fastest growing applications for computers and storage to support the growth of new applications using the Internet, like IPTV (Internet Protocol TV.) Data centers need extremely high speed connections so they generally use either special coax cables or optical fiber at 10 Gb/s. The electronics to drive UTP cable at these speeds takes considerably more power than fiber or coax (5-10X), primarily for the sophisticated digital signal processing to reduce signal distortion on twisted pairs. TIA has developed standards for data center cabling (TIA 942) that address this demanding application.

UTP Cabling For Networks

The standard UTP cable used to connect networks has 4 pairs of wires. The first generation of networks using UTP needed only two pairs, one transmitting in each direction, and Fast Ethernet managed to work on two pairs on the higher performance of Category 5 cable with 100 MHz bandwidth. But when Gigabit Ethernet was developed, it was necessary to use all four pairs simultaneously in both directions, as well as requiring a further development of Cat 5 specifications. 10G Ethernet went even further, requiring additional development of Cat 6 cable to 500 MHz bandwidth and even tighter specifications, to work even when using all 4 pairs.

Network	Minimum Cable Rating	Pairs Used
10 Base-T (Ethernet)	Category 3	2, 3
Token Ring (4 Mb/s)	Category 3	1,3
Token Ring (4 Mb/s)	Category 4	1,3
100 Base-TX (Fast Ethernet)	Category 5	2,3
1000 Base-T (Gigabit Ethernet)	Category 5e	All pairs, bidirectional
10G Base-T (10 Gigabit Ethernet)	Category 6A	All pairs, bidirectional

Some applications that do not require high bandwidth or crosstalk isolation can use splitters to allow two systems to share one cable. A typical application is two 10 Base-T links or an Ethernet link and a phone line.

All networks have versions that operate over optical fiber as well as UTP. Fiber is generally the medium of choice for network backbones at speeds of Gb/s or higher. Most premises networks use multimode fiber but now some installations use designs similar to fiber to the home (FTTH), passive optical network (PON) systems, that run over singlemode cabling.

Home networks have been developed that operate over power lines and CATV coax. These options are generally used when a home is connected to broadband and cabling that supports PC networks is needed inside the home, but the owner does not want to install new cabling.

Power over Ethernet (PoE)

The IEEE 802.3 Ethernet committee created a standard for powering network devices such as wireless access points, VoIP phones and surveillance cameras off the spare pairs in a 4-pair UTP cable. The standard was developed since Ethernet up to 100Base-TX, used only pairs 2 and 3, pairs 1 and 4 are available to provide power. Pair 1 (pins 4/5) is the + conductor, pair

4 (pins 7/8) is the - conductor. This method is now known as Mode B. Mode A uses pairs 2 and 3, the same pairs used for data transmission, for powering network devices that have been designed to implement PoE standards.

PoE uses a 48 volt power supply and requires cable of Cat 5 rating or higher. Almost 13 watts of power are available in IEEE 802.3af, 25W in IEEE 802.3at, adequate for powering VoIP phones or many wireless access points, thus saving cabling costs. Power may be delivered using what are called midspan devices, dedicated PoE power supplies that can be plugged into links or even provide patch panel capability as well or endspan devices, typically switches designed to provide power as well as function as an Ethernet switch.

PoE has a long development period toward standardization, so like many other standard systems, numerous "pre-standard" system implementations exist, not all of which are compatible. Some devices and applications may use more power than available from standard systems (as much as 60 watts) and some cables may not be capable of carrying full power without excess heating. Generally, PoE does not affect the design or installation of UTP cable but the cabling designer must be careful to understand what devices are being considered for use on the cabling to ensure compatibility.

Fiber Optics In Structured Cabling

While UTP copper has dominated premises cabling, fiber optics has become increasingly popular as computer network speeds have risen to the gigabit range and above. Most large corporate or industrial networks use fiber optics for the LAN backbone cabling. Some have also adopted fiber to the desktop using a centralized fiber architecture which can be quite cost effective. Even fiber to the home architectures are being used in premises networks.

Fiber offers several advantages for LAN backbones. The biggest advantage of optical fiber is the fact it can transport more information longer distances in less time than any other communications medium. In addition, it is unaffected by the interference of electromagnetic radiation which makes it possible to transmit information and data through areas with too much interference for copper wiring with less noise and less error; for example: in industrial networks in factories. Fiber is smaller and lighter than copper wires which makes it easier to fit in tight spaces or conduits. A properly designed centralized fiber optic network may save costs over copper wiring when the total cost of installation, support, regeneration, etc. are included.

Replacing UTP copper cables to the desktop with fiber optics was generally not cost effective, as each link requires media converters to connect to the copper port on the PC to fiber and another on the hub/switch end unless dedicated hubs/switches with fiber ports are used. Some users did that, as they expected to upgrade to speeds that would not run on UTP and did not want to install upgrades each time the network speed increased.

However, the solution to cost-effective fiber in the LAN is using centralized fiber. Since fiber supports longer links than copper, it's possible to build networks without telecom rooms for intermediate connections, just passive fiber optics from the main equipment room to the work area. In the standards, this is known as centralized fiber architecture. Since the telecom room is not necessary, the user saves the cost of the floor space for the telecom room, the cost of providing uninterrupted power and data ground to the telecom room and year-round air conditioning to remove the heat generated by high speed networking equipment. This will usually more than offset the additional cost of the fiber link and save maintenance costs.

Virtually every network standard has an option for fiber optics, often more than one to take advantage of different fiber characteristics and the extreme distance capability of optical fiber. Appendix C has a listing of networks using fiber and their specifications.

Passive Optical LANs

An alternative to structured cabling has developed from the fiber to the home (FTTH) passive optical network (PON) architecture. FTTH has grown rapidly to now connecting tens of millions of homes worldwide. As a result of its manufacturing volume and unique passive splitter design, the PON has become extremely inexpensive to connect users with voice, data and video over the same network. In 2009, PONs began appearing in corporate networks. Users were adopting these networks because they were cheaper, faster, lower in power consumption, easier to provision for voice, data and video, and easier to manage, since they were originally designed to connect millions of homes for telephone, Internet and TV services.

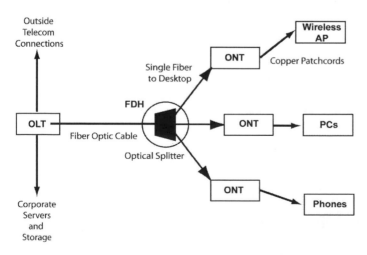

Like fiber to the home, the key element in the POL is the optical splitter in the fiber distribution hub (FDH) that allows up to 32 users to share the electronics in an OLT (optical line terminal), greatly reducing the system costs. The ONT (optical network terminal) connects to the network over a single fiber and acts as a media converter, connecting phones over conventional copper cables as POTs lines or VoIP and connecting PCs and wireless access points over standard Cat 5e/6 copper patchcords. *See Appendix B*

Fiber or Copper - or Wireless?

LAN cabling is often perceived as the big battleground of fiber versus copper, but in reality the marketplace has changed. The network user, formerly sitting at a desktop computer screen with cables connecting their computer to the corporate network and a phone connected with another cable, is becoming a relic of the past.

People now want to be mobile. Practically everybody uses a laptop, excepting engineers or graphic designers at workstations, and most of them will have a laptop as a second computer to carry, along with everybody else, to meetings where everybody brings their laptops and connects on WiFi. When was the last time you went to a meeting where you could connect with a cable? Besides laptops on WiFi, people use Blackberries and iPhones for wireless communications. Some new devices, like the iPhone, allow web browsing with connection over either the cellular network or a WiFi network. Some mobile phones are portable VoIP devices connecting over WiFi to make phone calls. While WiFi has had some growing pains and continual upgrades, at the 802.11n standard, it has become more reliable and offers what seems to be adequate bandwidth for most users.

The desire for mobility, along with the expansion of connected services, appears to lead to a new type of corporate network. Fiber optic backbone with copper to the desktop where people want direct connections and multiple wireless access points, more than is common in the past, for full coverage and maintaining a reasonable number of users per access point is the new norm for corporate networks.

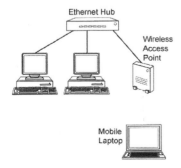

What about fiber to the desk? Progressive users may opt for FTTD, as a complete fiber network can be a very cost effective solution, negating the requirement for telecom rooms full of switches, with data quality power and grounds, plus year-round air conditioning. Power users, like engineers, graphics designers and animators can use the bandwidth available with FTTD. Others go for a zone system, with fiber to local small-scale switches, close enough to users for those who want cable connectivity instead of wireless, to plug in with a short patchcord.

It's the job of the designer to understand not only the technology of communications cabling, but also the technology of communications, and to keep abreast of the latest developments in not only the technology but the applications of both.

Further Study
Review the premises cabling topics on the FOA Online Reference Guide at www.foaguide.org

Review Questions

True/False
Indicate whether the statement is true or false.

_____ 1.   If the network does not require high bandwidth, it can share the 4 pairs in a UTP cable to transmit 2 Ethernet signals or one Ethernet and one voice line.

Multiple Choice
Identify the choice that best completes the statement or answers the question.

_____ 2.   Ethernet was first developed as a _____ architecture using _____ cable with _____.
     A. Bus, coax, taps
     B. Bus, UTP, RJ-45 connectors
     C. Star, UTP, RJ-45 connectors
     D. Ring, coax, RJ-45 connectors

_____3.   The development of _____ provided a low cost cabling
          alternative for networks.
          A. CATV coax
          B. IBM Type 1 cable
          C. Balanced transmission on UTP cabling
          D. Ethernet

_____4.   FDDI and Token Ring networks used a _____architecture.
          A. Bus
          B. Star
          C. Ring
          D. Balanced

_____5.   Ethernet changed from a _____ to _____ network architecture
          when it switched to UTP cable.
          A. Bus, ring
          B. Bus, star
          C. Ring, coax
          D. Ring, UTP

_____6.   Even _____ require cabling connections in a network.
          A. Wireless access points
          B. Mobile phones
          C. Laptop computers
          D. Blackberries

_____7.   Until Gigabit Ethernet, LANs only used _____ pairs of the UTP
          cable.
          A. 1
          B. 2
          C. 3
          D. 4

_____8.   Gigabit Ethernet uses all four pairs of a UTP cable _____.
          A. For power
          B. With 2 pairs in each direction
          C. Bidirectionally
          D. Simultaneously and bidirectionally

_____9.   Hardware like video cameras designed to run on coax can be used on UTP with a converter device called a _____.
A. Splitter
B. Balun
C. Adapter
D. TOSLINK

Additional Study and Projects

Use the web to find out more about networks including Ethernet and legacy networks such as Token Ring, FDDI, ESCON, Arcnet, WangNet and DecNet. Find out how Ethernet standards have been developed by the IEEE 802.3 committee. Where do the other network standards come from? Learn more about the history of cabling that these networks used.

Chapter 4
Copper Cabling

Objectives: From this chapter you should learn:
How UTP cable is used to transmit signals for communications
Grades of UTP cable
Termination of UTP cable
Testing UTP cabling systems
How coax cable cable is used in premises cabling systems

Unshielded Twisted Pair

Because computer networking evolved over several decades, many different cabling solutions have been used. But today, virtually all premises copper cabling in the US with the exception of TV cables has moved to unshielded twisted pair (UTP) as specified in the EIA/TIA 568 standard (ISO/IEC 11801 worldwide) because it has been inexpensive, may already be in place, is familiar to installers and is simple to install. The cost and simplicity of installation has changed a bit, however, with higher performance grades like Cat 5e/6/6A. Some users, mostly outside the US, use shielded twisted pair (STP) with shields over each pair in the cable or screened twisted pair (ScTP) with an overall shield around all the pairs. These cables can provide higher performance but require more care in installation.
UTP cable has been a standard cable for telephone systems for almost a century, where it is generally used for analog phone systems (POTS or plain old telephone service.) These cables are generally large multipair cables with pair-count configurations of 25, 50, 100, 200 pairs or more.

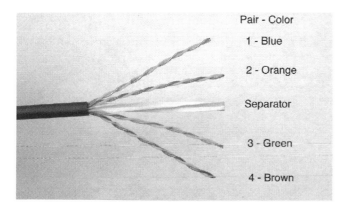

Pair - Color

1 - Blue

2 - Orange

Separator

3 - Green

4 - Brown

Most UTP cable used in structured cabling systems today is comprised of four pairs of carefully twisted pairs of solid copper wire, insulated with carefully chosen material to provide high bandwidth, low attenuation and crosstalk. Cables permanently installed in premises cabling systems use solid wire for higher performance but patchcords generally use stranded wire for greater flexibility and ruggedness when handled.

UTP cable works so well because it is used with transmitters that work on "balanced transmission" as shown below. They transmit equal but opposite signals on each wire of the pair so each wire has only half the amplitude of the final signal. The electrical and magnetic fields of each wire are opposite and cancel out each other, producing low electromagnetic emissions. Likewise, electromagnetic pickup is the same on both wires so they cancel out. The twists on the pair of wires mixes the emissions from the electrical signals so they cancel out.

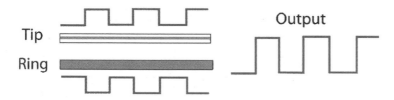

Twisted Pair Trivia: The two wires are referred to as "tip" and "ring" - but why? Does it have something to do with the ringer on a phone? No! It refers to the connection on a old phone plug from manual switchboards. The white/stripe wire was connected to the "tip" of the plug and the solid wire to the "ring" connector behind it!

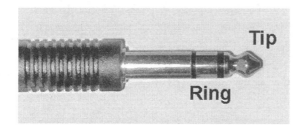

The secret ingredient of Cat 5e/6 is the twists of the pairs! Below, you can see the difference in the twists in each pair for different types of cables. From the left, we have telephone wire with hardly any twists in the pairs, then Category 3, Category 5e and Category 6 cables, with each higher grade having more tightly twisted pairs. The Cat 6 cable even has a separator between the pairs to reduce crosstalk at the higher frequencies where it will be used.

The pairs are twisted tightly and very consistently, but each pair is twisted at a different rate to "tune" them to different frequencies to prevent crosstalk

between the pairs. In order to maintain Cat 5e/6/6A performance, especially crosstalk, you absolutely must keep the twists as close as possible to the terminations- no more than 1/2 inch - 13 mm should be untwisted!
UTP cable is terminated mostly in jacks, connector receptacles that have punchdown terminations on the backside and twists in the connectors inside to prevent crosstalk. See Terminations. Some snap into work area outlets, others are incorporated in rack mount patch panels. 568 allows many possible cable configurations, including intermediate punchdowns, but a direct run from a work area outlet to a patch panel will provide the highest performance, likely necessary if upgrades to fast networks like Gigabit Ethernet are contemplated.

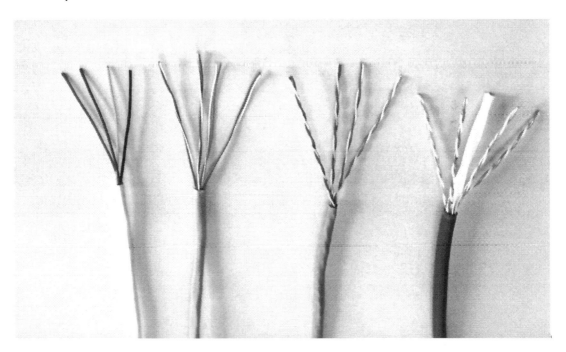

Patchcords for connecting network equipment to the outlet or patchpanel are usually purchased factory-assembled. The connector (plug) is properly called a "modular 8 pin connector" but usually is referred to as a RJ-45, which is actually a specific telco pin configuration on the same plug. They use stranded cable for flexibility and require special connectors. Order them to proper length if you can to prevent the mess that patch panels often become after a few moves and changes.

Performance Grades
Higher performance UTP cables were developed as computer network speeds increased and needed higher bandwidth cables. The first graded cable, Cat 3 was adequate for 10 Megabits/s Ethernet or 4 Mb/s Token Ring. Token ring at 16 Mb/s required higher performance cable, so Cat 4 was introduced, but neither network nor cable grade lasted long. Instead Cat 5

was introduced to support "Fast Ethernet" at 100 Mb/s.

When Ethernet was upgraded to 1 gigabit per second (1000 Mb/s) , Cat 5 was upgraded to "enhanced" Cat 5 or Cat 5e. Cat 6 was developed by cable manufacturers as a higher performance cable with more headroom, but no network was ever specified to use it. Instead, when 10 Gb/s Ethernet was developed, an "augmented" Cat 6, Cat 6A, was required.

In Europe, a shielded cable, Class F is used. Some US manufacturers offer a version of this cable they call "Cat 7" but TIA has not considered this cable part of TIA-568, so "Cat 7" is not its proper nomenclature. However, TIA is considering adding "Cat 8" as a higher speed cable for limited distance links in data centers.

You can get hardware and cable rated for Cat 3, Cat 5e, Cat 6 or Cat 6A. With cable, it's easy to see the difference; it's in the twists - higher performance cables have more twists. Jacks are harder to tell the differences, but they are different. Inside jacks rated Cat 5 or above, you will find internal twists to reduce crosstalk inside the jack itself. If you terminate Cat 5e cable with Cat 3 jacks, you will get Cat 3 performance - no better! When dealing with high performance UTP cabling like Category 5e, Cat 6 and Cat 6A designed to support Gigabit Ethernet or faster, termination procedures become even more complicated! It's vitally important to ensure all components are rated to the same high level in order to achieve that performance level.

Instead of the "Categories" used in the US, in Europe and much of the rest of the world they use "Classes" to designate performance. Here's a table of performance and correllations to US standards. (Remember these are the standards which specify minimum performance, so many manufacturers will offer cables with frequency performance greater than the standards for competitive reasons.)

ISO/IEC Class	US Category	Frequency (MHz)
A		0.1
B		1
C	3	16
D	5e	100
E (EA)	6 (6A)	250 (500)
F (FA)	7 * (7A)	600 (1000)

* Not currently under consideration by TIA as a US standard

Here's a guide to the differences in the categories for UTP cables:

EIA/TIA(ISO)	Cat 5	Cat 5e (Class D)	Cat 6 (6A) (Class E, EA)	"Cat7" (7A) (Class F, FA)
Supports networks	100Base-T	1000Base-T	1000Base-T (10Gbase-T)	? None currently considered
Test Frequency	100 MHz	100MHz	250 MHz (500 MHz)	600 MHz (1000 MHz)
Length	100 meters	100 meters	100 meters	100 meters
RJ-45 Compatible	yes	yes	yes	No
Field Tester Requirement:	Level 2	Level 2e	Level 3 (3e)	Unknown

Other Twisted Pair Cable Types

Like everything else that deals with computers and communications, the speed of networks is going up. Cat 5e is adequate to handle one gigabit/ second networks, but the EIA/TIA TR 42 committee approved a new standard for Cat 6 cabling in June of 2002 after three years of debate, discussion and testing. Unfortunately, during that time network speeds jumped to 10 Gigabits/ second, requiring another redesign, leading to "augmented Cat 6" or Cat 6A.

Each new standard includes cables, plugs and jack, patch panels and patch cords, in other words, everything you need to install a complete cabling system since. Performance specifications for Cat 6A are for significant advances over Cat 6 or Cat 5e - with attenuation and crosstalk performance higher at every level.

So using higher rated cables give you more "headroom" - better signal to noise ratios - which can mean more robust data transmission on slower Fast Ethernet and Gigabit Ethernet (1000base-T) networks.

Cat 6 never had a real reason for existence but many people installed it as a higher performance cable than Cat 5e. Gigabit Ethernet ran fine on Cat 5e (some manufacturers say it runs well on Cat 5 now) and when 10 Gigabit Ethernet came along, it could initially only run on fiber optics. The copper suppliers would not allow their product to be bypassed by technology, so an "augmented" Cat 6 was spec'ed for 10GbE with approval in March, 2008. The problem with Cat 6A seems to be not within the cable itself, but in crosstalk with adjacent cables, called "alien" crosstalk and the high power consumed by Cat 6A transceivers to send such high speed signals over copper. Fiber remains the most reliable solution for GbE and above.

This leap in technological advances, like all previous ones, comes with a cost. The goal of the committee is that each generation of Category-rated cable be "backward compatible" which means that any networking product that works on Cat 3, 5 or 5e is supposed to work on Cat 6. The other issue that the group wrestles with is "interoperability" - mixing and matching components. This part of the standard states that cable plant containing mixed categories (eg: Cat 5e patchcords on a Cat 6 cabling systems) is supposed to work without compatibility issues, but will only work at the level of the minimum component specification (Cat 5e in this case).

Finally, there is the issue of compatibility among different manufacturers products. Practically everybody, including the manufacturers, told users installing "pre-standard" Cat 6 to stick to one manufacturer's products or those tested for compatibility. The EIA/TIA press release on the Cat 6 standard stated: "To ensure generic cabling system performance, Category 6 component requirements are specified to be interoperable when products from different manufacturers are mated". The same issue probably exists with Cat 6A.

The Europeans have a standard called Class F - a shielded 600 MHz cabling system. The EIA/TIA TR42 committee has declined to consider such a standard in the US due to lack of interest from the network development committees.

Internationally, ScTP and STP cable is much more common, as concerns over electromagnetic interference have affected standards more than in the US. ScTP cable is simply a UTP cable with a metallic foil shield over all 4 twisted pairs. Some manufacturers also call it FTP for foil-shielded twisted pair. The foil shield is for noise immunity, keeping outside noise out of the pairs and keeping emissions from the pairs themselves from escaping the cable. ScTP is not the same as shielded twisted pair which has a foil shield over each individual pair and may also have a shield over all the shielded pairs under the cable jacket.

Current ScTP cables are smaller than most UTP cables that are rated as Cat 6A (augmented Category 6). The problems of crosstalk between pairs in two separate cables that affects Cat 6A, called alien crosstalk, is negated by the foil shield of ScTP. For UTP Cat 6A cables, the solution to alien crosstalk was bigger cables with thicker jackets, causing problems with the number of cables that could be accommodated in conduits and cable trays. ScTP Cat 6A cables are no larger than Cat 6 UTP cables, making them easier to fit in current cabling hardware.

For termination, ScTP cables use shielded modular 8-pin connectors just like UTP but with a shield. Terminating the shield is pretty simple, just like adding a 9th wire to the cable. One does have to worry about grounding, as ScTP cable must be tied into the grounding busbar in the telecom room along with all the racks and other metallic hardware.

The extra conductor in the cable offers another benefit. It can be used for cable management systems where it allows tracking cable connections using add-on electronic equipment that automates the most time consuming part of any cabling project – keeping documentation up to date.

Cable Listings For Flammability

All cables installed inside buildings must meet flammability requirements of the building and electrical codes, which in the US means the NEC (National Electrical Code) or CEC in Canada. Communications cable will be rated per the following table, depending on its use:

Cable Designation	Application
CMX	General use for dwellings and raceways
CMR	Riser rated for use in vertical shafts, rated to prevent carrying fire from floor to floor
CMP	Plenum rated for use in environmental air spaces such as dropped ceiling spaces used for air return

CATV cable (CATV) and multipurpose cable (MP) are also covered under other sections of the electrical codes.

Network Cable Handling

The performance of the cabling network is heavily dependent on the quality of the installation. The components used in structured cabling installation have been carefully designed and exhaustively tested to meet or exceed the requirements of EIA/TIA 568 for performance at 100 MHz. If the cable is not properly installed, performance will be degraded. In particular, one should avoid bending the cable too tightly, kinking it or using tightly installed cable ties which can crush the cables. Loosely bundling cables with "hook and loop" cable ties is much better. (See Chapter 8: Installation for more tips.)

UTP Cable Termination

UTP cables are terminated with standard connectors (plugs and jacks) or punchdowns. The plug/jack is often referred to as a "RJ-45", but that is really a telco designation for the "modular 8 pin connector" terminated with a USOC pinout used for telephones. The male connector on the end of a patchcord is called a "plug" and the receptacle on the wall outlet is a "jack."

These terminations are called "IDC" for "insulation-displacement connections," since the wires are held in knife-edge terminations that slice through the insulation and dig into the copper wire, forming a tight seal like this.

All IDC connections require untwisting a small amount of each pair to get the wires into the contacts. In order to minimize crosstalk and return loss problems, its necessary to keep the amount of wire in each pair untwisted and minimize the amount of cable jacket removed. For Cat 5/5e/6/6A cable, the maximum amount of untwisted wire is specified as 0.5" (13 mm) but it's good practice to minimize the amount of untwist and the length of cable jacket removed.

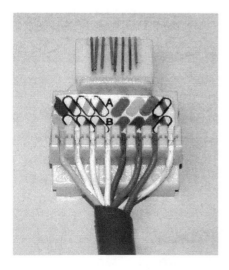

Connector Pinouts and Color Codes

In structured cabling as specified by TIA-568, there are two possible color codes or pinouts, called T568A and T568B which differ only in which color coded pairs are connected - pair 2 and 3 are reversed. Either work equally well, as long as you don't mix them! If you always use only one version, you're OK, but if you mix A and B in a cable run, you will get crossed pairs! While it makes no difference electrically which one you use, it is not wise to use both in one customer location. Always check to see which scheme has been used and continue using that one in new cabling installation.

The cable pairs are color coded as shown:

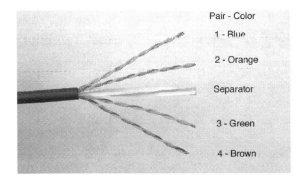

Each pair consists of a colored wire and a white wire with a matching color stripe. The stripe wire is "tip" and the solid color wire is "ring," referring to the tip of the old 1/4" telephone plug and the ring around the shaft that makes the connections.

Note: Plugs/jacks and punchdowns have different color codes! You cannot mix them up as they will result in wiremap errors - esp. split pairs which cause big problems with high speed transmission.

Jacks: The jacks are then terminated with these layouts, looking into the jack:

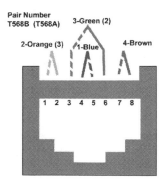

Note that the only difference between T568A and T568B is the reversal of pairs 2 and 3 - it's only a color code change.

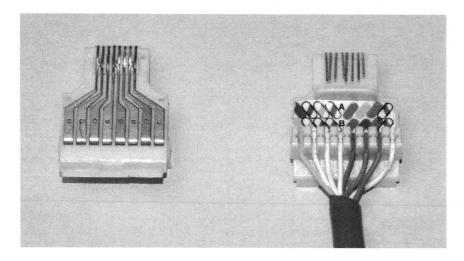

The color codes are going to look like this on a jack, showing both T568A and T568B termination schemes:

Note: Cat 3 jacks and all plugs are going to use these color codes shown above. However, Cat 5, 5e and 6 jacks have internal connections that continue the twists as close to the pins in the jacks as possible to maintain the performance level. Thus the pinout on the back of the jacks will not usually follow the standard color code layouts (see the pin sequence and the twists in the internal connections of the jack in the photo above).

Remember: Always follow the color codes on the back of the jacks to insure proper connections!

Terminating Jacks

Jacks usually have 110-style punchdowns on the back which can be terminated with a punchdown tool, using special manufacturer's tools or even a snap-on cover for the connector. Again, you MUST keep the twists as close to the receptacle as possible to minimize crosstalk.

Plugs: The plugs are terminated by straightening out the wires in proper order and crimping on a connector. Like we said before, you MUST keep the twists as close to the plug as possible to minimize crosstalk.

Patchcords: They generally use stranded wire for flexibility but can be made with solid wire for higher performance. Note that plugs may be different for each type of wire, so make sure you have the right type.

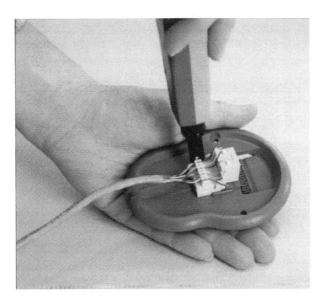

Crossover Cables: Normal cables that connect a PC/NIC card to a Hub are wired straight through. That is pin 1 is connected to pin 1, pin 2 to pin 2, etc. However, if you are simply connecting two PCs together without a hub, you need to use a crossover cable made by reversing pair 2 and 3 in the cable, the two pairs used for transmisson by Ethernet. The easy way to make a crossover cable is to make one end to T568A color coding and the other end to T568B. Then the pairs will be reversed.

Punchdowns

Sometimes there are cross connects using punchdowns in the telecom closet, more common on telephone wires than data. These are called punchdowns because the cable is punched down into the IDC contacts with a special tool, called (surprise!) a punchdown tool. Of course, you MUST keep the twists as close to the punchdown as possible to minimize crosstalk.

Punchdowns come in 4 varieties: 110, 66, Bix and Krone. Most popular for LAN interconnects is the 110 block. For telephone cables with large pair counts (25, 50, 100, etc.), the 66 block is the most common. The Bix and Krone blocks are rarer proprietary designs (Bix from Northern Telecom, Krone from Krone in Germany) are used mostly on the manufacturer's own installations.

Here is a 110 block as used in LAN interconnects and on UTP jacks. The actual IDC contacts are in the connecting block that is punched down on the base, sandwiching one cable, then the second cable is punched down on the top.

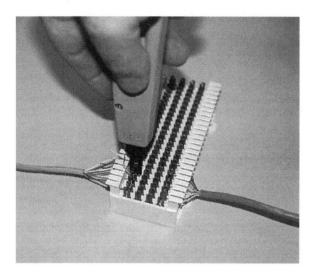

66 block as used for POTS (plain old telephone system) telephone systems. They are designed for interconnecting large pair count cables. There are four rows of punchdown IDC contacts. One cable is punched down on the outside row of contacts of each side then the two sides are connected using the inside rows of contacts. If connections are directly across, bridging clips can be used. Otherwise, bridging wire is punched down on the correct contacts on each side to make connections.

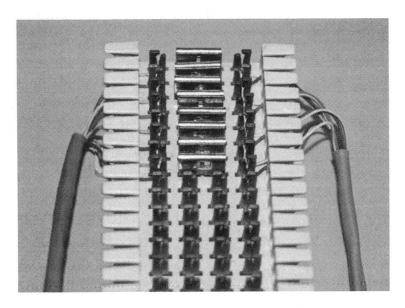

Color Codes For Punchdowns

Punchdowns of all types are always made with the pairs in order with the white/stripe wire (tip) first, then the solid colored wire (ring).

Pair 1(w/blue-blue)
Pair 2 (w/orange-orange)
Pair 3 (w/green-green)
Pair 4 (w/brown-brown)

(This color code is often remembered by BLOG - BLueOrangeGreen and brown is all that's left!)

Refer to our online "virtual hands-on" explanation of the termination processes of Cat 3/5/5E/6 for complete illustrated procedures (www.foaguide.org).

Patch Panels

Patch panels offer the most flexibility in a telecom closet. All incoming wires are terminated to the back of the patch panel on 110-style punchdowns (again watching the 1/2 inch limit of untwisting pairs). Then patch cables are used to interconnect the cables by simply plugging into the proper jacks.

Patch panels can have massive number of cables, so managing these cables can be quite a task in itself. It is important to keep all cables neatly bundled and labeled so they can be moved when necessary. However, it is also important to maintain the integrity of the cables, preventing kinking or bending in too small a radius which may adversely affect frequency performance.

One should also avoid bundling the cables too tightly. Crushing the cables can affect the performance, since it can affect the twist and pair alignment in the cable which affects high frequency performance. If one uses regular plastic cable ties, they should be tightened only finger tight and cut off - do not use cable tie guns which may tighten tight enough to damage the cables. Preferably use "hook and loop" cable ties which have an added advantage that they can easily be opened to add or remove cables.

Testing UTP Cabling

Since Cat 5e/6/6A UTP cable is used to the fullest extent of its performance envelope, comprehensive performance testing is very important. There are three basic tests that are called for as part of the EIA/TIA-568 specs for all UTP cables: wiremap, length and high speed performance. We'll take a look at each of them and equipment needed to test them.

What Is A "Certified" Cable?

Certification has been used by vendors of testers to mean that the cable was tested and passed by one of the Cat 5e/6/6A "certification" testers which test all the standard's specified performance parameters. It means that the cabling meets the minimum specifications of EIA/TIA standards and should work with any network designed to operate on a Cat 5e/6 link.
Thus, a "certification tester" or "certifier" is an instrument that tests the cabling and compares it to the TIA-568 standards, certifying that the cable meets the minimum performance specifications required by the standard.

What is "Verification"?

Alternatively, cable may be tested to determine if it will carry the network signals intended for use on the cabling systems. These testers run network bit error rate tests (BERT) over the cable as well as checking wiremaps and length. A "cable verifier" will guarantee the cabling will support Gigabit Ethernet, for example, but does not test to the TIA cabling standards, only a problem if some other usage, such as analog video, may be used.

Wiremap

Wiremapping is a simple test that confirms that each wire is hooked up correctly, with no opens or shorts. UTP intended only for POTS (plain old telephone service) voice applications actually only needs to be tested for wiremap. Wiremapping is very straightforward. Structured cabling standards do not consider simple voice grade cable, only cable of Categroy 3 or above, so most cable testing will require more than just wiremapping. Each pair must be connected to the correct pins at the plugs and jacks, with good contacts in the terminations. A "wiremapper" is basically a continuity checker that determines if pins are correctly connected.

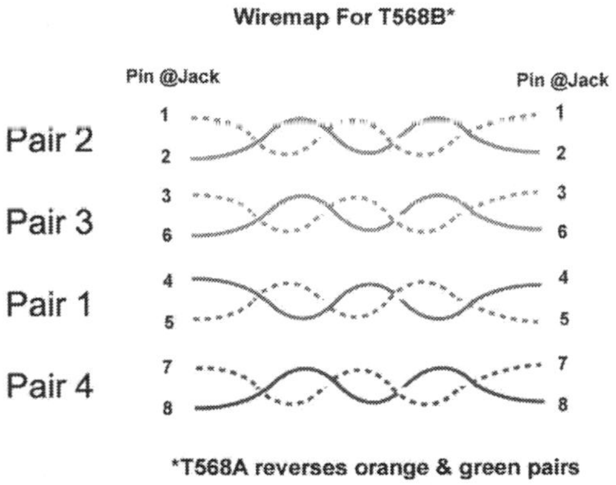

Wiremap For T568B*

Pin @Jack   Pin @Jack

Pair 2 — 1, 2

Pair 3 — 3, 6

Pair 1 — 4, 5

Pair 4 — 7, 8

*T568A reverses orange & green pairs

Most of the failures are simple enough to understand, like reversed wires in a pair, crossed pairs, opens or shorts. One possible failure, crossed pairs, is caused when both wires of a pair are crossed at one termination. The usual cause of a crossed pair is a 568A termination on one end and a 568B on the other.

The most difficult wiremap problem is a split pair, when one wire on each pair is reversed on both ends. It causes the signal to be sent on one wire each of two pairs. The usual DC wiremap will pass but crosstalk will fail. It takes a more sophisticated wiremapper or Cat 5e/6/6a tester to find a split pair, as some wiremappers which use only DC tests do not check crosstalk. In our experience, a split pair is usually caused by someone using punchdown color codes on jacks which splits the pairs.

Here are examples of wiremap faults. Compare the diagrams to the correct one above to see the wiring errors.

Shorts and Opens
Shown here, pair 2 (orange) is open because tip is not connected.
Pair 3 (greeen) is shorted on pin 6.

Wiremap For T568B* - Short or Open

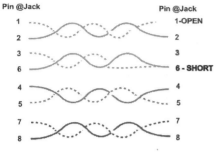

*T568A reverses orange & green pairs

Reversed Pairs
Pair 3 (green) has tip and ring reversed.

Wiremap For T568B* - Reversed Pair

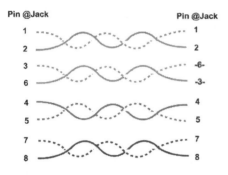

*T568A reverses orange & green pairs

Transposed or Crossed Pairs
Pair 2 (orange) and pair 3 (green) are crossed, connected to each others pins. The usual cause of crossed pairs is one end is terminated at T568B and the other end T568A, where pairs 2 and 3 are reversed.

Wiremap For T568B*
Transposed or Crossed Pairs

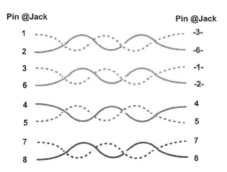

*T568A reverses orange & green pairs

Split Pairs

Split pairs are when one wire of each pair is improperly connected. Here pairs 1 (blue) and 3 (green) are connected such that a DC wiremap tester will test OK, but the signals are being carried on one wire of two pairs, so the cables are unbalanced. Split pairs are often caused by the wires being punched down on a jack using the color codes for punchdown blocks.

Length

Since 568 cables must be less than 90 meters (296 feet) in the permanent link and 100 meters in the channel (328 feet), cable length must be tested. This is done with a "time domain reflectometer" (TDR) which is a cable "radar". The tester sends out a pulse, waits for a reflection from the far end and measures the time it took for the trip. Knowing the speed of the pulse in the cable (calibrated for various cable types), it calculates the length. All cable certification or verification testers include a TDR to measure length.

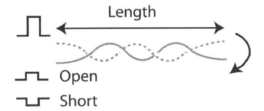

Besides measuring length, the TDR looks at the polarity of reflected pulses to find shorts or opens. If you have a short or open, the TDR will tell you what and where the problem is by looking at the return pulse, making it a great tool for troubleshooting problems. If the return pulse is the same polarity, the cable is open. If the pulse is of opposite polarity, the cable is shorted. If no return pulse is seen, the cable is terminated at its characteristic impedance.

Performance Testing For Certification

Performance testing for attenuation, crosstalk, etc. requires testing over the full frequency range of the cable. The frequency range for each cable type is:

Cat 3: 16 MHz
Cat 5/5e: 100 MHz
Cat 6: 250 Mhz
Cat 6A: 500 MHz

Attenuation

The proper operation of a LAN on the cable plant requires the signal strength be high enough at the receiver end. Thus the attenuation of the cable is very important. Since LANs send high speed signals through the cable and the attenuation of the cable is variable with the frequency of the signal, certification testers test attenuation at many frequencies specified in the 568 specs.

Attenuation

This test requires a tester at each end of the cable, one to send and one to receive, then one of them will calculate the loss and record it. There are pass fail criteria for the cable at Cat 3, 4, 5, 5e, 6 and 6A max frequencies. Here is how a typical cable attenuation changes with frequency.

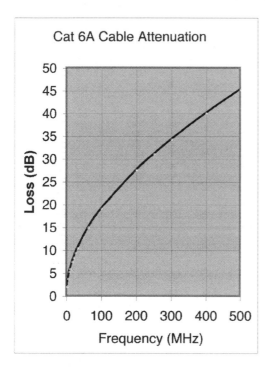

Crosstalk (NEXT)

It's called NEXT for "near end cross talk" since it measures the crosstalk (signal coupled from one pair to another) at the end where one pair is transmitting (so the transmitted signal is largest causing the most crosstalk.) Crosstalk is minimized by the twists in the cable, with different twist rates causing each pair to be antennas sensitive to different frequencies and hopefully not picking up the signals from it's neighboring pairs. Remember what we've said repeatedly: you MUST keep the twists as close to the terminations as possible to minimize crosstalk.

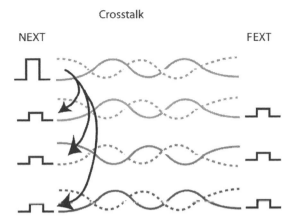

Cat 5e /6 testers measure crosstalk from one pair to all three other pairs for each pair and compare it to the 568 specs, giving a pass/fail result. Some also calculate "ACR" or attenuation/crosstalk ratio, as it is a measure of how big the crosstalk signal is to the attenuated signal at the receiver. You want this number as big as possible, as it is an indication of the signal to noise ratio.

Tests on Cat 5e/6 for Gigabit Ethernet

The additional test specs for Category 5e and 6 includes a number of new tests to insure higher performance from the cable to make it compatible with Gigabit Ethernet. These tests relate to higher bandwidth usage of the cable and simultaneous use of all four pairs in both directions at once.

Powersum Crosstalk (NEXT) is the NEXT on one pair when all three others are carrying signals. This is realistic with 1000Base-T Gigabit Ethernet where all pairs carry signals simultaneously.

Far End Crosstalk, looking at the effect of the coupling from one pair to another over the entire length, is measured at the far end. As tested, it's ELFEXT or equal level FEXT, or the ratio of FEXT to attenuation, similar to ACR.

Delay Skew measures how much simultaneous pulses on all 4 pairs spread out at the far end. This measures the speed on each pair, which may be different due to the variations in number of twists (more twists means longer wires) or insulation. Since 1000Base-T Gigabit Ethernet uses all 4 pairs with the signals split into 4 separate signals, it's necesary to have all arrive simultaneously. Testers measure Propagation Delay, the actual transit time on the pairs to calculate Delay Skew.

Delay Skew

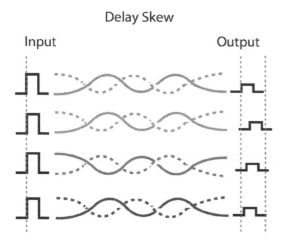

Input   Output

Return Loss is a measure of the reflections from the cable due to variations in the impedance. These reflections can cause signal degradation, especially if the pairs are used in a full-duplex (bidirectional) mode. With 1000Base-T Gigabit Ethernet transmitting in both directions on each pair, return loss can cause big problems.

Requirements For Testing Cat 6/6A For 10Gigabit Ethernet

The development of augmented Cat 6 (Cat 6a) cable for use on 10 Gigabit Ethernet links added a new test. The cable is so precisely made, especially the rate of twist in the pairs, that cable pairs can interfere with the same pair in other cables nearby. This added a new test for Cat 6A which is called "Alien Crosstalk".

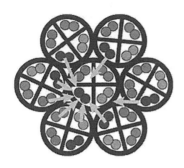

Performing this test is time consuming and is highly dependent on the physical location of cables. Some controversy regarding the relevance of this test exists in the industry, with some cabling vendors not requiring it.

Cable Testers

Wiremappers test the connections and Cat 5e/6 certification testers test the performance at high frequencies. Cable Certifiers test the cable according to TIA-568 standards. Cable Verifiers test the cable to see if it will transmit Ethernet signals without errors.
Cable Certification Testers are mostly automated, "push a button get a pass/fail" simple. Certification testers test everything, wiremap, length, attenuation and crosstalk in one connection, give you a pass/fail result, help on troubleshooting and store the result for printing reports for the customer.

Some installers use the certification tester for all testing, after the cable is installed. But it's a very expensive unit that needs a trained operator and many failures are simply wire map problems. Others have each crew use an inexpensive wiremapper to make sure all connections are correct before the certification tester is brought in. By having each crew find and fix their own wiremap problems, testing and corrections are done as the cable is installed and the cost of the certification tester is not wasted on simple problems. It's just provides the high frequency tests and documentation required by most users.

Cable Verifiers are a new class of testers that use the Ethernet communications protocols to ensure the cable supports the system intended for use on it, generally a LAN or connection to a wireless access point.

Since some UTP cables are used for non-Ethernet applications like CCTV, security or building management systems that are designed to operate on TIA-568 standardized cabling, a certification tester may be a better choice for them.

Permanent Link Adapters

The tester's adapter interface cable may be the weakest link when testing. Conventional adapter cords may be the cause for many false failures in the field. Susceptible to the daily wear and tear associated with rough field conditions, they degrade with time and contribute to return loss, crosstalk and attenuation.

Until now, each tester used personality modules specific to each manufacturer's Cat 6/6a cabling for testing. The personality modules insured that the connection between the adapter and the link under test yield optimum performance and more valid tests.

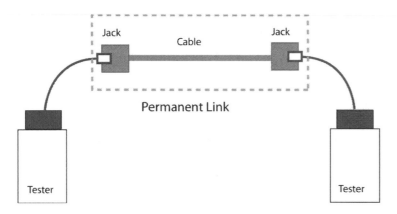

A change in the definition of the "link" was implemented in EIA/TIA568 B and ISO 11801 AM2 and it is now called the "permanent link." The permanent link moves the test reference point to the end of the test cable at the wall outlet or patch panel jack, including only the connector on the end of the tester interface cable.

Coax Cables In Premises Cabling Systems

Coaxial cable has always been the mainstay of high speed communications, being supplanted by twisted pair wiring primarily by cost considerations. Coax was used for the cabling of the first computer networks, ARCnet and Ethernet for it's bandwidth capability, until UTP with balanced transmission techniques was developed and fiber optic options became available. Today, most video, both CATV (community antenna TV) and CCTV (closed circuit TV) are carried inside premises over coax, although much surveillance CCTV is over fiber at longer distances and some is now carried on UTP cabling using adapters. Coax has also returned to networking for use with 10 gigabit links in data centers (10Gbase-CX4) because of low cost for short (<10m) links.

Coax Cable

Coaxial Cable Construction

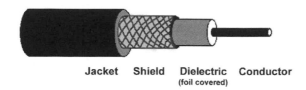

Jacket   Shield   Dielectric   Conductor
(foil covered)

The design of coax cable gives it the high bandwidth capability. The center conductor carries the signal down the middle of the cable, held in place and insulated by a plastic dielectric. The outer conductor is the signal ground and acts as a shield to contain the signal inside the cable. Signal leakage is big problem in CATV where the high frequency signals can cause interference in many electronic devices. A coax signal is a simple modulated voltage, allowing simpler transceivers than UTP where signal processing is needed to remove problems like crosstalk and reflections. The cable has a characteristic impedance, usually 50 or 75 ohms, so transmitters must be selected to be appropriate to the characteristics of the coax cable being used.

Types of Coax Cable

There have been a number of types of coax cables developed over the history of electronics and communications. Most are referred to by the designation "RG" which stands for "Radio Guide," an old American military term from the name of the book, and a number, which was the number of the page in the standards book on which specifications were written. Here are some of the more common cables currently in use.

Early computer networks used 50 ohm coax, both regular Ethernet (Thicknet, standardized as 10Gbase-5) which used a special version of RG-8 and ThinNet on RG-58 (also called "cheapernet" and standardized as 10Gbase-2.) RG in RG-8, remains the way most people refer to coax, although "Series-6" is the preferred term today. Thicknet used type "N" connectors and a clamp-on "tap" to connect devices to the cable with an interface converter, while cheapernet used BNC connectors and BNC tees for connections.

RG Number	Impedance (Ohms)	Center Conductor (AWG)	Cable Diameter (in/ mm)	Applications
RG-6	75	18	0.275/6.99	CATV, Satellite TV, CCTV
RG-8	50	10	0.405/1.03	Ethernet 10Base-5, Amateur Radio
RG-8X	50	19	0.242/6.15	Amateur Radio
RG-11	75	14	0.405/1.03	Low loss for video
RG-58	50	24	0.195/4.95	Ethernet 10Base-2, Other legacy LANs
RG-59	75	20	0.242/6.15	CCTV, video

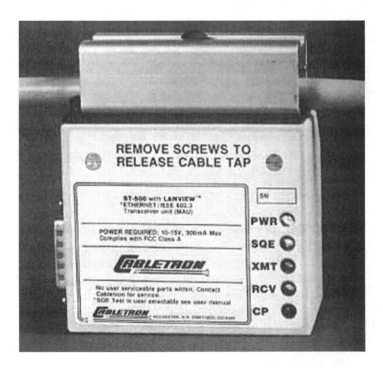

10Base-5 Tap with AUI (Attachment Unit Interface)

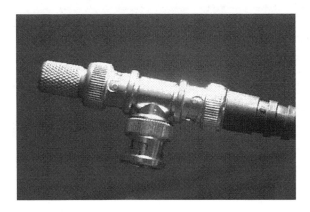

10Base-2 with BNC "T" connector

Computer networking has not abandoned coax. The standards for data center environment recognizes the use of coaxial cables for specific types of circuits. The coaxial cables recognized are 75-ohm cables using BNC connectors. The 10 gigabit Ethernet has a standard using coax, 10Gbase-CX4, using a multiple coax cable and standard connector shown below which is also used for storage networks in the Infiniband standard.

10Gbase-CX4

Video uses 75 ohm cable. Most CCTV video uses either the BNC connector and RG-59 cable or a "F" connector with RG-6 (shown below) as is used for CATV and satellite TV. The F connector is inexpensive and easy to install since the cable center conductor is hard and can be used as the center pin of the connector.

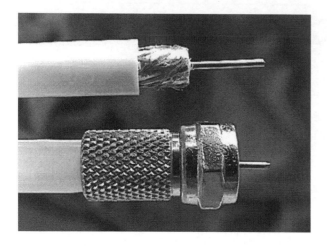

Trivia: the center conductor of the RG-6 CATV cable is made of steel coated in copper. The higher conductivity of copper is not needed, since the high frequency of TV signals (~100 MHz) causes the signal to remain on the surface of the conductor, called the "skin effect." Satellite TV, however, uses the center conductor for power and needs the lower resistance of an all-copper conductor, plus it uses higher frequency cable.

Installation

Coax cables can be installed in a similar manner and in similar locations to other copper and fiber optic cables. Coax is pulled in conduit, laid in cable trays above the ceiling or under the floor or lashed to hooks like other communications cables. Like all cables, coax cables need to be installed carefully, as overstressing by pulling by too much tension or kinking the cable can cause transmission problems. Likewise, after installation, it should not be crushed by heavy weights being placed on it.

Termination

All coax terminations are performed in a similar manner. Here is the process for terminating RG-6 with an F connector:
Strip center conductor
Strip jacket
Roll back shield
Push on connector (or crimp on connector)
Crimp
Alternate: Screw-on connectors can be used but are not generally recommended as they are prone to signal leakage. The cable is stripped then the connector is screwed onto the cable with a screwdriver-like device or T-handle.

BNC connectors require a center pin to be crimped or soldered to the center conductor of the cable after stripping but before sliding the connector on the cable.

Terminating a F-type Connector

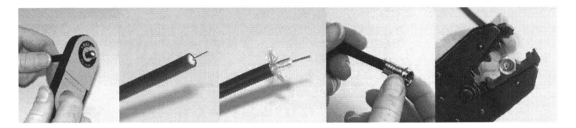

Stripping coax for termination is a 2 step process that requires a special coax cable stripper. Many types of coax strippers are available. Most use adjustable blades for the two cuts, as this cut is done deeply, while the second cut is much shallower. Some like the one shown below strips to different depths from each side while others strip differently depending on the direction of rotation around the cable.

Strip everything down to the center conductor using a coax cable stripper to expose 3/8 inch (~10 mm) of center conductor

Second Strip - Jacket Only
Set stripper blade to cut through only the jacket but not damage shield braid. This may require making several test cuts and adjusting the coax stripper blade Peel off jacket, exposing the braided shield

Fold the braided shield back over the jacket to contact the connector body. The "pin" formed by the center conductor is visible. The foam dielectric in the cable holds the center conductor/pin in place.

Push the connector on the cable to the proper depth, where the pin should protrude slightly.

Crimp with the die size specified for the connector. Some connectors require two crimps, one close to the nut that is larger and a smaller one on the cable.

Testing Coax

Generally, installers only test coax cable continuity with ohmmeter or coax cable tester. You can loop it to test from one end with a terminator or a clip lead. Problems associated with coax termination include:

Opens: no contact on connector shell, the braid did not get crimped to the shell properly.

Shorts: braid wire contacts center conductor. Stray wires from the braid may get twisted around the center conductor, shorting the cable. Check closely for all braid wires before putting the connector on.

Kinking of coax cable sometimes causes uneven frequency response, especially at higher frequencies, which can only be found with sophisticated frequency test equipment. Severe kinks require replacement of the cable.

Further Study
Review the premises cabling topics on the FOA Online Reference Guide at www.foaguide.org

Review Questions

Multiple Choice
Identify the choice that best completes the statement or answers the question.

_____1.   What do UTP Category 3, Category 5e and Category 6 designations indicate?
    A. The frequency performance grade of the cable
    B. UL-rated Flame retardence of the cable
    C. How far the cable will work in networks
    D. They are trade names for cable types

_____2.   What minimum level of UTP cable type is required by 1000Base-T (Gigabit Ethernet)?
    A. Cat 5
    B. Cat 5e
    C. Cat 6
    D. Augmented Cat 6

_____3.   What is the <u>main</u> characteristic of unshielded twisted pair Category 5e or Category 6 cable that gives it high frequency performance?
    A. High performance plastics in the insulation of the pairs
    B. The size of the conductors
    C. The rate of twists in the pairs of wires
    D. The connectors

_____4.   Category 6A cable is specified and must be tested during
          certification to _____ MHz.
          A. 100
          B. 250
          C. 500
          D. 1000

_____5.   The name for the latest generation Cat 6 UTP cable for use with
          10 Gigabit networks is _____.
          A. Enhanced Cat 6
          B. Extended Cat 6
          C. Augmented Cat 6
          D. Cat 7

_____6.   If you use an Cat 3 UTP jack on newer Cat 5e cable plant, the link
          performance will meet _____specs.
          A. Cat 3
          B. Cat 5
          C. Cat 5E
          D. Cat 6

_____7.   Before UTP cabling became widely used and the industry
          standard, most Ethernet Networks were connected over _____
          cable.
          A. Copper
          B. Coaxial
          C. Shielded
          D. Telephone

_____8.   Standard UTP (unshielded twisted pair) copper cabling for voice
          and data installations has how many pairs of wire?
          A. Two
          B. Three
          C. Four
          D. Twenty-five

_____9.   Attenuation in copper cable_____.
          A. Is lower at higher frequencies
          B. Is higher at higher frequencies
          C. Is the same at all frequencies
          D. Is highest at 10 MHz

_____10.   When terminating Cat 5e/6, what must be remembered to maintain the performance of the installed cable?
A. Keep the pairs twisted to within 1/2 inch of the termination
B. Do not strip insulation off the wires
C. The jacket of the cable must not be stripped back more than 3 inches
D. The punchdown tool must cut off the wires close to the end

_____11.   Why are punchdown blocks used with Cat 3 and Cat 5 cabling?
A. Terminate cables from equipment
B. Interconnect cables in a telecom closet
C. Change from T568A to T568B terminations
D. Meet EIA/TIA 568 Standards

_____12.   Which punchdown block is more often used with data (Cat 5e/6)?
A. Bix block
B. Krone block
C. 110 block
D. 66 block

_____13.   Which punchdown block is more often used with POTS telephone connections?
A. Bix block
B. Krone block
C. 110 block
D. 66 block

_____14.   What kinds of connection to the cable does a UTP jack typically have?
A. 66 punchdown
B. 110 punchdown
C. Snap-in contacts
D. Solder connections

_____15.   Does a jack have the same color code for the pairs as a punchdown block?
A. No
B. Yes
C. Depends on the type and manufacturer of the jack
D. Depends on whether it is T568A, T568B or USOC

_____16.   The Cat 3 jack is the same as a Cat 5e/6 jack except _____.
            A. There are no internal twists to enhance performance
            B. The punchdowns fit bigger wires
            C. It only connects to RJ-45 plugs
            D. It is keyed to snap into outlets upside down

_____17.   What is a RJ-45 connector?
            A. The connector used only with Cat 5e/6 jacks
            B. A special high frequency connector
            C. A modular 8 pin connector with USOC pinout
            D. A trade name

_____18.   The difference between the termination schemes of T568A and
            T568B is _____?
            A. Keying on plugs and jacks
            B. Reversal of tip and ring
            C. Reversal of pairs 2 and 3
            D. Determined by the speed of the network

_____19.   What is a "certified" UTP cable?
            A. Cable tested to EIA/TIA 568 specifications
            B. Cable tested by an automated tester
            C. Cable tested to both Cat 3 and Cat 5 specifications
            D. Cable tested to "enhanced Cat 5" or "augmented Cat 6"
               specifications

_____20.   What instrument measures the length of a cable?
            A. Network analyzer
            B. Wiremapper
            C. Time domain reflectometer (TDR)
            D. All of the above

_____21.   Why is "Powersum NEXT" important in new cable plants?
            A. Higher speed networks need less crosstalk
            B. New networks have signals on all the pairs in the cable
            C. Cat 5e and Cat 6 cable are more sensitive to crosstalk
            D. It's a marketing issue, not a technical issue

_____22.   What is included in a channel test that is not included in a
           permanent link test?
           A. Patchcords on either end of the link
           B. Extra attenuation from the connections at the ends
           C. Longer cable lengths
           D. Performance of the networking equipment

_____23.   What is the most likely cause of crossed pairs?
           A. Misreading color codes on a Cat 3 jack
           B. Terminating one end as T568A and the other as T568B
           C. Using a Cat 3 jack on one end and a Cat 5e/6 jack on the
              other
           D. Termination of the jack using the BLOGBr color code
              sequence

_____24.   Voice grade unshielded twisted pair cables (UTP) which are only
           intended to carry POTS (plain old telephone service) only need
           testing for_____.
           A. Shorts and opens
           B. Wiremap
           C. Crossed pairs
           D. Crosstalk

_____25.   Of the three copper testers, (wiremappers, certification and the
           new validation testers), which actually tests the cable for real
           networks like Ethernet?
           A. Wiremapper
           B. Certification tester
           C. Validation tester
           D. None of them

Additional Study and Projects
Use the FOA Online Reference Guide (www.foaguide.org) to learn more
about copper cable installation and termination. See how to terminate cables
using the virtual hands-on (VHO) tutorials.
Learn how to install and terminate copper cables in a hands-on lab. Learn
how twisted pair cable is punched down on 110 and 66 blocks (BIX and Krone
also if available) and how cable is terminated in plugs and jacks.

Chapter 5
Fiber Optic Cabling

Objectives: From this chapter you should learn:
How fiber optics is used in premises cabling
The types of fiber and cable
Terminating fiber optic cables
Testing fiber optic cables

The Role of Fiber Optics In Premises Networks

While UTP copper has dominated premises cabling, fiber optics has become increasingly popular as computer network speeds have risen to the gigabit range and above. Most large corporate or industrial networks use fiber optics for the LAN backbone cabling. Some have also adopted fiber to the desktop using a centralized fiber architecture which can be quite cost effective. Even fiber to the home architectures are being used in premises networks as passive optical LANs. *See Appendix B*

Backbones

Fiber offers several advantages for LAN backbones. The biggest advantage of optical fiber is the fact it can transport more information longer distances in less time than any other communications medium. In addition, it is unaffected by the interference of electromagnetic radiation which makes it possible to transmit information and data through areas with too much interference for copper wiring with less noise and less error; for example: in industrial networks in factories. Fiber is smaller and lighter than copper wires which makes it easier to fit in tight spaces or conduits. A properly designed centralized fiber optic network may save costs over copper wiring when the total cost of installation, support, regeneration, etc. are included.

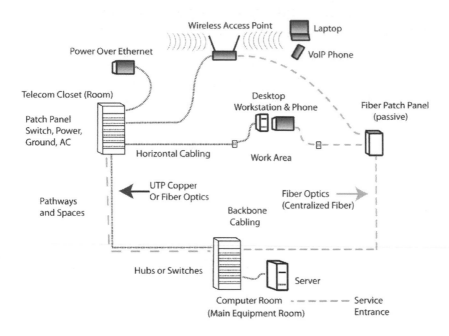

Centralized Fiber To The Desktop

Replacing UTP copper cables to the desktop with fiber optics was never cost effective, as each link requires converters to connect to the copper port on the PC to fiber and another on the hub/switch end unless dedicated hubs/switches with fiber ports are used. Some users did pay that cost, as they expected to upgrade to speeds that would not run on UTP and did not want to install upgrades each time the network speed increased.

However, the solution to cost-effective fiber in the LAN is using centralized fiber (see right side of diagram above). Since fiber supports longer links than copper, it's possible to build networks without telecom rooms for intermediate connections, just passive fiber optics from the main equipment room to the work area. In the standards, this is known as centralized fiber architecture. Since the telecom room is not necessary, the user saves the cost of the floor space for the telecom room, the cost of providing uninterrupted power and data ground to the telecom room and year-round air conditioning to remove the heat generated by high speed networking equipment. This will usually more than offset the additional cost of the fiber link and save maintenance costs.

Other Premises Uses For Fiber

Premises cabling for LANs is where the fiber/copper/wireless arguments generally focus. A century and a half of experience with copper communications cabling gives most users a familiarity with copper that makes them skeptical about any other medium. And in many cases, copper has proven to be a valid choice. Most building management systems use proprietary copper cabling; for example: thermostat wiring, as do paging/ audio speaker systems. Security monitoring and entry systems, certainly the lower cost ones, still depend on copper, although high security facilities like government and military installations often pay the additional cost for fiber's more secure nature.

Surveillance systems are becoming more prevalent in buildings, especially airports, government offices, banks, casinos or other buildings that are considered possible security risks. While coax connections, common in short links and structured cabling, can run cameras limited distances on Cat 5E or Cat 6 UPT like computer networks, fiber has become a much more common choice. Besides offering greater flexibility in camera placement because of its distance capability, fiber optic cabling is much smaller and lightweight, allowing easier installation, especially in older facilities like airports or large buildings that may have available spaces already filled with many generations of copper cabling.

Industrial networks have used fiber for many years. In a factory environment, immunity from the electrical noise generated by machinery is often the primary reason for using fiber instead of copper cables. The long distances in large buildings and the need to have small cables that can easily be pulled in conduit also argue for fiber's use.

A Quick Fiber Primer

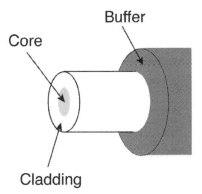

Optical fiber is comprised of a light carrying core surrounded by another optical layer called the cladding that traps light into the core. Fiber is characterized by the size and composition of the core which determines how the light is carried in the core.

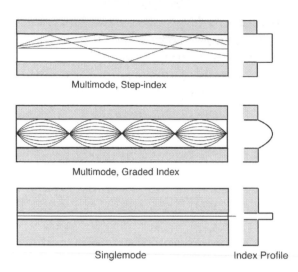

Multimode, Step-index

Multimode, Graded Index

Singlemode   Index Profile

Step index multimode fiber has a core comprised of one single type of optical material, either glass or plastic. It has higher attenuation and is too slow for many uses, due to the dispersion caused by the different path lengths of the various modes travelling in the core. Step index fiber is not widely used - only POF (plastic optical fiber) and PCS/HCS (plastic or hard clad silica, plastic cladding on a glass core) use a step index design today.

Graded index multimode fiber uses variations in the composition of the glass in the core to compensate for the different path lengths of the modes. It offers hundreds of times more bandwidth than step index fiber - up to about 2 gigahertz. Two types are in use, 50/125 and 62.5/125, where the numbers represent the core/cladding diameter in microns.

Singlemode fiber shrinks the core down so small that the light can only travel in one ray. This increases the bandwidth to almost infinity - but it's practically limited to about 100,000 gigahertz - that's still a lot! Singlemode fiber has a core diameter of 8-10 microns, specified as "mode field diameter," the effective size of the core, and a cladding diameter of 125 microns.

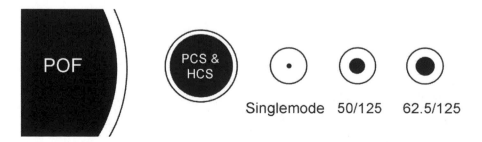

POF   PCS & HCS   Singlemode   50/125   62.5/125

Most premises cabling is multimode fiber but some backbones use singlemode for telecom or CATV signals. Multimode fiber comes in several sizes, defined by its core size and bandwidth specs. For many years premises applications primarily used 62.5/125 multimode fiber, originally called "FDDI fiber" because the first fiber-only LAN used it, but now internationally standardized as OM1 fiber. With the advent of Gigabit Ethernet and Fibre Channel at gigabit speeds, the low bandwidth capability of OM1 fiber with 850 nm VCSEL laser sources used for gigabit transmitters limited it's link lengths, so many users switched to 50/125 fiber which had been optimized for 850 nm lasers in the earliest days of fiber optics for telephone links. OM2 fiber had good bandwidth, but manufacturers developed OM3 fiber with even higher bandwidth and longer link capability. OM3 is generally the fiber of choice for premises LAN use today, but even higher bandwidth 50/125 fiber, called OM4, is in development.

Fiber optic transmission systems all use data links that work similar to the diagram shown above. Each fiber link consists of a transmitter on one end of a fiber and a receiver on the other end. Most systems operate by transmitting in one direction on one fiber and in the reverse direction on another fiber for full duplex operation. It's possible to transmit both directions on one fiber but it requires couplers to do so and fiber is less expensive than couplers. A FTTH passive optical network (PON) is one of the only systems using bidirectional transmission over a single fiber because its network architecture is based around couplers already.

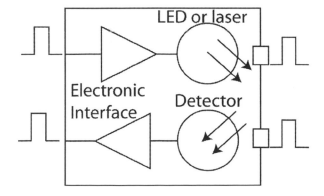

Most systems use a "transceiver" which includes both transmission and receiver in a single module. The transmitter takes an electrical input and converts it to an optical output from a laser diode or LED. The light from the transmitter is coupled into the fiber with a connector and is transmitted through the fiber optic cable plant. The light from the end of the fiber is coupled to a receiver where a detector converts the light into an electrical signal which is then conditioned properly for use by the receiving equipment.

Data Link Performance And Link Power Budget

Measuring Data Transmission Quality
Just as with copper wire or radio transmission, the performance of the fiber optic data link can be determined by how well it transmits data; how well the reconverted electrical signal out of the receiver matches the input to the transmitter.

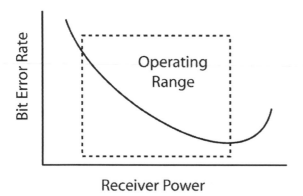

The ability of any fiber optic system to transmit data ultimately depends on the optical power at the receiver as shown above, which shows the data link bit error rate as a function of optical power at the receiver. (BER is the inverse of signal-to-noise ratio, e.g. high BER means poor signal to noise ratio.) Either too little or too much power will cause high bit error rates. Too much power, and the receiver amplifier saturates, too little and noise becomes a problem as it interferes with the signal. This receiver power depends on two basic factors: how much power is launched into the fiber by the transmitter and how much is lost by attenuation in the optical fiber cable plant that connects the transmitter and receiver.

Link Power Budget
The optical power budget of the link is determined by two factors, the sensitivity of the receiver, which is determined in the bit error rate curve above and the output power of the transmitter into the fiber. The minimum power level that produces an acceptable bit error rate determines the sensitivity the receiver. The power from the transmitter coupled into the optical fiber determines the transmitted power. The difference between these two power levels determines the loss margin (power budget) of the link.

High speed links like gigabit or 10gigabit Ethernet LANs on multimode fiber have derating factors for the bandwidth of fiber caused by the dispersion spreading out the digital data pulses. Older 62.5/125 OM1 fiber will generally operate only on shorter links while links on 50/125 OM3 laser-optimized fiber will go the longest distance.

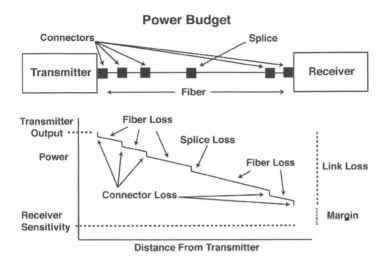

Which Fiber?

Premises networks are quite different from long-haul outside plant systems. Long haul systems use singlemode fiber which has the lowest attenuation and virtually unlimited bandwidth. Premises cabling distances are short so attenuation of the fiber is of less concern, although bandwidth can be a major issue with gigabit networks and faster.

Early, and slower, premises systems used LED sources with 62.5/125 micron (called OM1) fibers (and 100/140 in the earliest LANs), but LEDs are not useable above about 250 Mb/s. With the advent of Gigabit Ethernet and the faster versions of Fibre Channel, premises networks switched to transmitters using 850 nm VCSELs, vertical cavity surface-emitting lasers, that offered adequate speed at a very low cost.

Above 1 Gb/s, fiber bandwidth became an issue, as the distance limitation was fiber. With the advent of Gigabit Ethernet, fiber manufacturers brought back an older fiber design, 50/125 micron (now called OM2 fiber), that had higher bandwidth since it was originally designed for use with lasers around 1980. Further recent developments of 50/125 fiber has provided extremely high bandwidth capability (OM3 and OM4 fiber.) Most current networks use OM3 or OM4 fiber for new installations as it provides adequate bandwidth for future 10 gigabit networks.

Networks at 40-100 Gb/s on multimode fiber. are using parallel transmission with 4-10Gb/s or 10-10Gb/s links in parallel to provide the bandwidth. However many users prefer to use wavelength-division multiplexing on singlemode fiber with 4 wavelengths at 25 Gb/s.

Since many premises networks already have 62.5/125 fiber systems, adding

50/125 for new systems requires not mixing them, as connecting 62.5/125 fiber to 50/125 fiber will cause large mismatched fiber diameter losses. Color coding the 50/125 fiber in aqua per the standards is one good way to distinguish them. Another solution is to use LC connectors on OM2/OM3 systems which are not intermateable with ST or SC connectors commonly used on OM1 fiber cables.

Fiber Optic Cable Choice

Unlike UTP copper cables which are all 4-pair cables, fiber optic cables can be chosen with different fiber counts and different cable types to allow choosing the optimum cable for the application.

Patchcords are made from simplex tight buffer cables. Equipment connection cords or even some short links will use zipcord which is just two simplex cables molded together.

Most premises cables, especially backbone cables, are of the distribution type, which has the highest fiber count for the smallest cable diameter. Distribution cables have buffered fibers that can be directly terminated and placed in patch panels.

Breakout cables are bundles of simplex cables in a common jacket. Breakout cable is the most rugged premises cable, easily terminated directly on each subcable which is protected and needs no patch panels or boxes for protection. It is ideal for industrial applications or in equipment rooms.

Loose tube cables are designed for outside plant environments where high pulling tension and moisture protection is needed. They are difficult to terminate because of the bare fibers inside the tubes and are rarely used indoors. Since their primary use is outdoors where they need jackets that are resistant to moisture, sun, etc. they are not generally rated for flame retardance and cannot be used indoors.

All premises cables must be rated for fire retardance per NEC Article 770. Cables are rated for general purpose use, riser rated (more fire retardant) or plenum rated (low emissions for use in air-handling areas.)
Zipcord

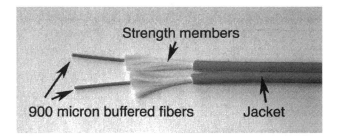

Distribution

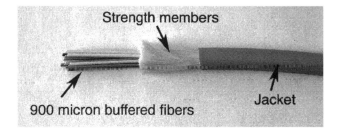

Loose Tube

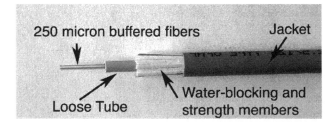

Breakout

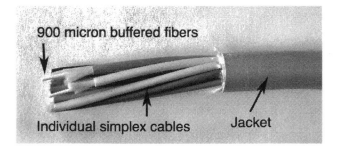

NEC Rating	Description
OFN	Optical fiber non-conductive

OFC	Optical fiber conductive
OFNG or OFCG	General purpose
OFNR or OFCR	Riser rated for runs between floors
OFNP or OFCP	Plenum-rated for use in air handling areas (plenums)
OFN-LS	Low smoke density

Cables without UL or other fire retardance markings should never be installed indoors as they will not pass building inspections! Outdoor cables are not fire-rated and can only be used up to 50 feet indoors. If you need to bring an outdoor cable indoors, consider a double-jacketed cable with PE jacket over a PVC UL-rated indoor jacket. Simply remove the outdoor jacket when you come indoors and you will not have to terminate at the entry point.

Color Codes

Fiber Type	Color Code		
	Non-military Applications(3)	Military Applications	Suggested Print Nomenclature
Multimode (50/125) (TIA-492AAAB) (OM2)	Orange	Orange	50/125
Multimode (50/125) (850 nm Laser-optimized) (TIA-492AAAC) (OM3)	Aqua	Undefined	850 LO 50 /125
Multimode (62.5/125) (TIA-492AAAA) (OM1)	Orange	Slate	62.5/125
Multimode (100/140)	Orange	Green	100/140
Single-mode (TIA-492C000 / TIA-492E000) (OS1, OS2)	Yellow	Yellow	SM/NZDS, SM
Polarization Maintaining Single-mode	Blue	Undefined	Undefined (2)

Most, but not all, premises fiber optic cables have jackets color-coded to indicate the fibers in the cable. Multimode cables are traditionally orange and singlemode are yellow. With the addition of OM2 and OM3 fibers to the mix,

OM3 cable jackets is color-coded aqua. The table below shows the color codes specifed in TIA-598.

Colored outer jackets or print may be used on Premises Distribution Cable, Premises Interconnect Cable or Interconnect Cord, or Premises Breakout Cable to identify the classification and fiber sizes of the fiber. When colored jackets are used to identify the type of fiber in cable containing only one fiber type, the colors shall be as indicated in Table. Other colors may be used providing that the print on the outer jacket identifies fiber classifications in accordance with subclause 4.3.3. Such colors should be as agreed upon between manufacturer and user.

Unless otherwise specified, the outer jacket of premises cable containing more than one fiber type shall use a printed legend to identify the quantities and types of fibers within the cable. Table 3 shows the preferred nomenclature for the various fiber types, for example "12 Fiber 8 x 50/125, 4 x 62.5/125." When the print on the outer jacket of premises cable is used to identify the types and classifications of the fiber, the nomenclature of the table is preferred for the various fiber types.

2 FIBER 62.5/125 FDDI (UL) c(UL) TYPE OFNR

Termination: Connectors and Splices

All fiber must have connectors which allow patching cables into links and connecting transmission equipment. Sometimes cables are permanently connected using splices, either fusion splices which are made by welding fibers together in an electrical arc or mechanical slices which have simple alignment fixtures that clamp fibers together. Connectors, not splices, are used in most premises cable plants, as their easy connection/disconnection/ reconnection offer the ability to reconfigure cable runs, test individual links and connect hardware where needed.

Fiber is terminated with connectors attached to individual fibers typically with one of three connector types, SC, ST or LC, or a dozen fibers at a time using MTP connectors. Connectors can be attached using adhesives and polished, prepolished connectors can be crimped onto the fibers or cables can be terminated in a factory and installed ready to use.

SC, ST, LC and MTP Connectors

Early structured cabling standards called for SC connectors as the standard, but users balked, as many had systems already installed with other types, primarily the ST. The standards committees then created the FOCIS documents (Fiber Optic Connector Intermateability Standard) and allowed the use of any connector with FOCIS documentation. Over time, many systems migrated toward the SC, but now the LC is gaining in popularity.

Most transceivers at 1 Gb/s or above use LC connectors for their smaller size and precision, making them a logical choice for cabling being used at high speeds. In addition, since newer cable plants are using 50/125 OM2 or OM3 fiber instead of the older 62.5/125 OM1 fiber for the higher bandwidth capability, using LC connectors on the OM2, OM3 and OM4 cable plants prevents mating 62.5/125 fiber to 50/125 fiber which can cause high excess loss from mismatched fibers when connecting the larger fiber to the smaller.

A multifiber connector, the MTP, has become more widely used for prefabricated cabling systems that have backbone cables which can be installed without termination and connect to patch panels with breakouts for single fiber connectors. These systems are factory made and require no field termination. MTP connectors are also used for parallel optics used in 40 and 100 Gb/s multimode links.

MTP Connector
Termination Procedures

Multimode connectors are usually installed in the field on the cables after pulling, while singlemode connectors are usually installed by splicing a factory-made "pigtail" onto the fiber. The tolerances on singlemode terminations are much tighter than multimode and the polishing processes are more critical, so singlemode termination is better done in a factory environment using polishing machines. You can install singlemode connectors in the field for low speed data networks, but you may not be able to get losses lower than 1 dB and reflectance may be a problem!

Connectors can be installed directly on most cable types, including jacketed tight buffer types like simplex, zipcord and breakout cables, where the aramid fiber strength members in the cable are crimped or glued to the connector body to create a strong connector. Connectors can be attached to the 900 micron buffered fibers in distribution cables, but the termination is not as rugged as those made to jacketed cables, so they should be placed in patch panels or boxes for protection. The 250 micron buffered fibers in loose tube cables cannot be easily terminated unless they have a reinforcement called a breakout kit or (furcation kit) installed, where each fiber is covered by a larger plastic tube. Generally loose tube and ribbon cables are terminated by splicing on a terminated pigtail.

Cables can be pulled with connectors already on them if, and a big if, you can deal with two issues: First, the length must be precise. Too short and you have to pull another longer one (its not cost effective to splice). Too long and you waste money and have to store the extra cable length. Secondly, the connectors must be protected. Some cable and connector manufacturers offer protective sleeves to cover the connectors, but you must still be much more careful in pulling cables. You might consider terminating one end and pulling the unterminated end to not risk the connectors. There is a growing movement to install preterminated systems with the MTP 12 multifiber connector. It's a very small connector, not much bigger than a ST or SC, but terminates up to 12 fibers. Manufacturers sell multifiber cables with MTPs on them that connect to preterminated patch panels with STs or SCs.

Multimode Terminations
Several different types of terminations are available for multimode fibers. Each version has its advantages and disadvantages, so learning more about how each works helps decide which one to use.

Singlemode Terminations
Singlemode fiber requires different connectors and polishing techniques

that are best done in a factory environment. Consequently most SM fiber is generally field terminated by splicing on a factory-terminated pigtail or prepolished/splice connector. Singlemode termination requires special connectors with much tighter tolerances on the ferrule, especially the hole for the fiber. Polishing requires special diamond polishing film on a soft rubber pad and a polishing slurry to get low reflectance. Factory terminated singlemode connectors are done using epoxy/polish techniques with machine polishing to get the proper endface finish needed for low loss and reflectance. You can put SM connectors on in the field if you know what you are doing, but expect higher loss and reflectance.

Adhesive Terminations

Most connectors use epoxies or other adhesives to hold the fiber in the connector ferrule and polish the end of the fiber to a smooth finish. Follow termination procedures carefully, as they have been developed to produce the lowest loss and most reliable terminations. Use only the specified adhesives, as the fiber to ferrule bond is critical for low loss and long term reliability! We've seen people use hardware store epoxies, Crazy Glue, you name it. And they regretted doing it. Only adhesives approved by manufacturers or other distributors of connectors should be used. If the adhesive fails, not unusual when connector ferrules were made of metal, the fiber will "piston" - sticking out or pulling back into the ferrule - causing high loss and potential damage to a mated connector.

The polishing process involves three steps but only takes a minute: "air polishing" to grind down the protruding fiber, polishing on a soft pad with the fiber held perpendicular to the polishing surface with a polishing puck and a quick final fine polish.

Epoxy/Polish

Most connectors, including virtually all factory made terminations, are the simple "epoxy/polish" type where the fiber is glued into the connector with epoxy and the end polished with special polishing film. These provide the most reliable connection, lowest losses (less than 0.5 dB) and lowest costs, especially if you are doing a lot of connectors. The small bead of hardened epoxy that surrounds the fiber on the end of the ferrule even makes the cleaving and polishing processes much easier - practically foolproof. The epoxy can be allowed to set overnight or cured in an inexpensive oven. A "heat gun" should never be used to try to cure the epoxy faster as the uneven heat may not cure all the epoxy or may overheat some of it which will prevent it ever curing. Don't use "Hot Melt" ovens either, as they use a much higher temperature and will ruin the epoxy.

"Hot Melt" Adhesive/Polish

This is a 3M trade name for a connector that already has the epoxy (actually a heat set glue) inside the connector. You insert the connector in a special oven. In a few minutes, the glue is melted, so you remove the connector, insert the stripped fiber, let it cool and it is ready to polish. Fast and easy, low loss, but not as cheap as the epoxy type, it has become the favorite of lots of contractors who install relatively small quantities of connectors. Remember you need a special Hot Melt oven, as it needs a much higher temperature than is used for curing epoxy.

Anaerobic Adhesive/Polish

These connectors use a quick setting "anaerobic" adhesive that cures faster than other types of adhesives. Various techniques of applying adhesive are used, including injecting it into the connector before inserting the fiber or simply wiping adhesive onto the fiber before inserting it in the connector. These adhesives dry in 5 minutes alone or in 30 seconds when used with a chemical accelerator.

Anaerobic connectors work well if your technique is good, but some do not have the wide temperature range of epoxies. A lot of installers are using Loctite 648, with or without the accelerator solution, that is neat and easy to use.

The Termination Process

For all types of adhesive/polish connectors, the termination process is similar. You start by preparing the cable, stripping off the outer jacket and cutting off strength members. Next you strip the fiber with a special tool that removes the plastic buffer coating without damaging the fiber. The fiber is then cleaned and set aside. Adhesive is applied to the connector or fiber and the fiber is inserted and crimped into the connector body.

After the adhesive is set, the fiber is then cleaved close to the end of the ferrule. Polishing takes three steps. First "air polish" to grind down the cleaved fiber to near the end surface of the ferrule. Then polish on two different grades of abrasive film placed on a rubber pad using a polishing puck to keep the fiber perpendicular to the surface.

Inspect the polished end of the connector ferrule with a fiber optic inspection microscope.

An experienced installer can terminate multifiber cables in about one minute per fiber, using the time required to cure the adhesive to prepare other connectors and reduce the time per connector.

It's important to follow termination procedures carefully, as they have been developed to produce the lowest loss and most reliable terminations. Use only the specified adhesives, as the fiber to ferrule bond is critical for low loss and long term reliability. And, like everything else, practice makes perfect!

Crimp/Polish
Rather than glue the fiber in the connector, these connectors use a crimp on the fiber to hold it in. Most types available in the past offered marginal loss performance and are thus no longer available. Expect to trade higher losses for the faster termination speed. A good choice if you only install small quantities and your customer will accept them.

Prepolished/splice (also called "cleave & crimp")
Some manufacturers offer connectors that have a short stub fiber already epoxied into the ferrule and polished and a mechanical splice in the back of the connector, so you just cleave a fiber and insert it like a splice, a process which can be done very quickly. Several connectors use a fusion splice instead of a mechanical splice to attach the connector.

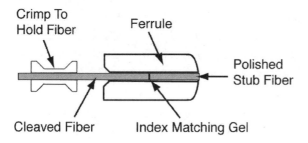

This method has both good and bad points. The manufacturing process is complex so these connectors are costly, as much as ten times as much as an adhesive/polish type, since they require careful manufacturing. Some of that extra cost can be recovered in lower labor costs for installation. You must have a good cleave on the fiber you are terminating to make them low loss, as the fiber cleave is a major factor in the loss of a mechanical splice. Using a high quality cleaver like those used for fusion splicing, available from some manufacturers as part of their termination kits, is recommended. Even if you do everything correctly, loss will be somewhat higher, because you have a connection loss plus a splice loss in every connector. The best way to terminate them is to verify the loss of the splice with a visual fault locator and "tweak" them as is done with mechanical splices.

Hints for field terminations
Here are a few things to remember when you are terminating connectors in
the field. Following these guidelines will save you time, money and frustration.

Whatever you do, always follow the manufacturer's termination instructions
closely.

Choose the connector carefully and clear it with the customer if it is anything
other than an epoxy/polish type. Some customers have strong opinions on
the types or brands of connectors used in their job.

NEVER take a new connector type in the field until you have installed enough
of them in the office or lab so that you know you can put them on successfully.
The field is no place to experiment or learn! One of the biggest cost factors
installing connectors is yield – how many pass testing. The biggest factor in
yield is the experience of the installer.

Have the right tools for the job. Make sure you have the proper tools in good
condition before you head out for the job. This includes all the termination
tools, cable tools and test equipment. Do you know your test cables are
good? Without that, you will test good terminations as bad every time. More
and more installers are owning their own tools like auto mechanics, saying
that is the only way to make sure the tools are properly cared for.

Dust and dirt are your enemies. It's very hard to terminate or splice in a dusty
place. Try to work in the cleanest possible location. Use lint-free wipes (not
cotton swaps or rags made from old T-shirts!) to clean every connector before
connecting or testing it. Don't work under heating vents, as they are blowing
dirt down on you continuously. Put covers on connectors and patch panels
when not in use. Keep them covered to keep them clean.

Don't overpolish. Contrary to common sense, too much polishing is just as
bad as too little. The ceramic ferrule in most of today's connector is much
harder than the glass fiber. Polish too much will cause undercutting of the
fiber and you create a concave fiber surface not convex as it should be,
increasing the loss. A few swipes is all it takes.

Change polishing film regularly. Polishing builds up residue and dirt on the
film that can cause problems after too many connectors and cause poor end
finish. Check the manufacturers' specs.

Inspect and test, then document. It is very hard to troubleshoot cables
when you don't know how long they are, where they go or how they tested

originally!

Do You Have To Terminate In The Field?

Many manufacturers offer prefabricated fiber optic cabling systems for both premises and outside plant systems. In fact, the largest application for prefabricated systems is fiber to the home (FTTH) where it saves a tremendous amount of time in installation and cost. Using prefab systems requires knowing precisely where the cable will be run so cable lengths can be specified. Using CAD systems and design drawings, a complete fiber optic cabling system is designed to the customer's specifications and built in a factory using standard components. Early prefabricated systems (some are still available) simply terminated cables with standard connectors like STs or SCs and protected them inside a plastic pulling boot with a pulling loop attached to the cable strength members. The cable would be installed with the boot in place then removed to connect into patch panels.

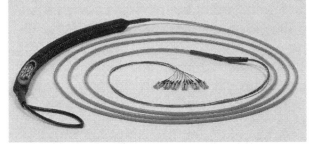

(Courtesy of Nexans)

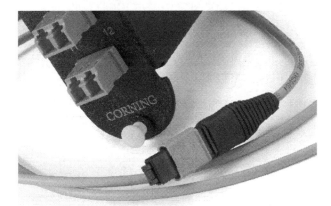

(Courtesy of Corning)

Today, it's more common to use backbone cables terminated in small multifiber MTP connectors that are pulled from room to room and connected to rack-mounted modules that have MTP connectors on the back and single fiber connectors on the front. Like everything else, there are tradeoffs. The factory-assembled connectors usually have lower loss than field terminations but the MTP connectors, even factory assembled, are not particularly low loss, so the total loss may be more than field terminated systems. Costs also involve tradeoffs, as factory systems are more expensive for the components but installation time is much less. In new facilities, considering prefabricated systems is always a good idea, but all factors should be considered before making a decision.

Managing and Protecting Terminations
While connectors are designed to be rugged enough to be handled and those terminating jacketed cables are fairly rugged, connectors still need some protection from damage. Since multifiber cables have many terminations where fibers may be accessed for testing or changing configurations, interconnection points require managing the terminations which includes identifying every connector/fiber end.
Connections can be made in many types of hardware including racks of patch panels or wall-mounted boxes. The proper types of hardware must be chosen appropriate to the installation.
Installation Issues
Fiber optic cable is, for the most part, installed in buildings the same way as copper wiring. Most cables are installed bare, without connectors, which are then installed in the field. Many installers feel that termination of fiber is no more difficult than Cat 6 copper, as installation techniques are not as likely to affect performance specs as termination of copper cables. These installers generally use traditional adhesive/polish termination procedures. The other choices for fiber termination are to use prepolished/splice connectors that use a simple prepare the cable and fiber, then crimp on the connector. Another option now considered both technically and economically viable is to install preterminated systems. These use factory-manufactured systems with miniature multifiber connectors that can be installed as easily as unterminated cables, but then only require plugging into breakout modules in a patch panel.

Fiber Optic Testing

Most premises cables are short enough that the primary cause of loss is the loss is the connectors, and, since they are generally field-terminated, connectors will be the focus of testing. Each connector should have three tests: 1) Visual inspection with a microscope to verify polishing if field polished and to ensure no dust or other contamination is present. 2) Loss, called insertion loss, measured by a light source and power meter. 3) Polarization, that is the fibers are arranged so one end of each fiber link is connected to a transmitter and the other end to a receiver.

Fiber testing is much simpler than copper or wireless testing, since the installation needs only testing for end-to-end loss with a simple fiber test set. Unlike copper, installation of connections is unlikely to affect the bandwidth of the fiber, only the loss, and fiber cables have no crosstalk problems, so simple loss testing is all that is required. Most premises networks are too short to be tested by OTDRs so OTDR testing is not required by any premises standard. Testing, therefore is simple, fast and inexpensive. Standards call for insertion loss testing using a light source and power meter with reference launch and receive cables which match the fiber size and connector type of the cable plant being tested as shown in the diagram below and described in TIA OFSTP-14.

Since most premises cables use multimode fiber, one must be careful to control the test source launch conditions in order to get trustworthy test results.

When the networking or transmission equipment is installed, an optical power meter can be used to test the transmitter and receive power in the link to determine if the system is withing the manufacturer's specifications.

Visual Connector Inspection by Microscope

Fiber optic inspection microscopes are used to inspect connectors to confirm proper polishing and find faults like scratches, polishing defects and dirt. They can be used both to check the quality of the termination procedure and diagnose problems. A well made connector will have a smooth, polished, scratch free finish and the fiber will not show any signs of cracks, chips or areas where the fiber is either protruding from the end of the ferrule or pulling back into it.

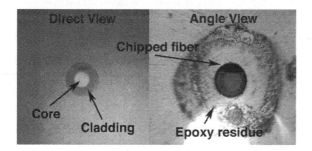

The magnification for viewing connectors can be 30 to 400 power but it is best to use a medium magnification. If the magnification is too low, critical details may not be visible. Inspecting with a very high magnification may cause the viewer to be too critical, rejecting good connectors. Multimode connectors should use magnifications in the range of 100-200X and singlemode fiber can use higher magnification, up to 400X. A better solution is to use medium magnification, but inspect the connector three ways: viewing directly at the end of the polished surface with coaxial or oblique lighting, viewing directly with light transmitted through the core, and viewing at an angle with lighting from the opposite angle or with quite oblique lighting. Viewing directly allows seeing the fiber and the ferrule hole, determining if the ferrule hole is of the proper size, the fiber is centered in the hole and a proper amount of adhesive has been applied. Only the largest scratches may be visible this way, however. Adding light transmitted through the core will make cracks in the end of the fiber, caused by pressure or heat during the polish process, visible.Viewing the end of the connector at an angle, while lighting it from the opposite side at approximately the same angle or using low-angle lighting and viewing directly will allow the best inspection for the quality of polish and possible scratches. The shadowing effect of angular viewing or lighting enhances the contrast of scratches against the mirror smooth polished surface of the glass.One needs to be careful in inspecting connectors, however. The tendency is to sometimes be overly critical, especially at high magnification. Only defects over the fiber core are generally considered a problem. Chipping of the glass around the outside of the cladding is not unusual and will have no effect on the ability of the connector to couple light in the core on multimode fibers. Likewise, scratches only on the cladding should not cause any loss problems.

The best microscopes allow you to inspect the connector from several angles, either by tilting the connector or having angle illumination to get the best picture of what's going on. Check to make sure the microscope has an easy-to-use adapter to attach the connectors of interest to the microscope.

Video readout microscopes are now available that allow easier viewing of the end face of the connector and some even have software that analyzes the finish. While they are much more expensive than normal optical microscopes, they will make inspection easier and greatly increase productivity.

Remember to check that no power is present in the cable before you look at it in a microscope to protect your eyes! The microscope will concentrate any power in the fiber and focus it into your eye with potentially hazardous results. Some microscopes have filters to stop the infrared radiation from transmitters to minimize this problem.

Testing Loss

There are two methods that are used to measure insertion loss with a light source and power meter, a "patchcord test" also called "single-ended loss," per TIA standard FOTP-171, and an "installed cable plant test" or "double-ended loss" per TIA standard OFSTP-14 (multimode) and OFSTP-7 (singlemode). The difference between the two tests is that single-ended loss testing uses only a launch cable and tests only the connector attached to the launch cable plus the fiber and any other components in the cable. Single ended testing is primarily used for testing patchcords or short cables since it can test each connector individually.

Double-ended loss testing uses a launch cable and receive cable attached to the meter and measures the loss of the connectors on both ends of the cable under test.

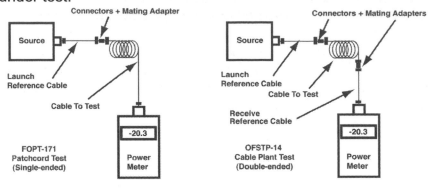

Single-ended testing is generally used on patchcords to allow testing the connectors on each end of a short cable individually to ensure both are good and allowing finding which connector might be bad if there is a problem. Double-ended testing is used with an installed cable plant to ensure the cable plant has been properly installed and to compare the test results to loss budget calculations.

Single-ended loss is measured by mating the cable you want to test to the reference launch cable and measuring the power out the far end with the meter. When you do this you measure only the loss of the connector mated to the launch cable and the loss of any fiber, splices or other connectors in the cable you are testing. Since you are aiming the connector on the far end of the cable at a detector on the power meter instead of mating it to another connector, it effectively has no loss so it is not included in the measurement. This method is described in FOTP-171 and is shown in the drawing. An advantage to this test is you can troubleshoot cables to find a bad connector since you can reverse the cable to test the connectors on the each end individually. When the loss is high, the bad connector is mated to the reference cable.

In a double-ended loss test, you attach the cable to test between two reference cables, one attached to the source and one to the meter. This way, you measure the losses of the connectors on each end, plus the loss of all the cable or cables, including connectors and splices, in between. This is the method specified in OFSTP-14 (multimode, the singlemode test is OFSTP-7), the standard test for loss in an installed cable plant.

Setting "0 dB" Reference For Loss Testing
In order to measure loss, it is first necessary to set a reference launch power for loss which becomes the 0 dB value. Correct setting of the 0 dB reference power is critical to making good loss measurements.
For single-ended testing, the reference power for 0 dB is set at the end of the reference cable. Simply attach the power meter to the end of the cable,

measure the output power and, with most meters, set that as the reference for loss measurements. The meter will then read the loss of each cable tested directly.

There are three methods of setting the reference for a double-ended test, using one, two or three reference cables, and the method chosen will affect the measured loss. Why are there three methods? The three methods developed because of the variations in connector styles and how test equipment is made.

Cleanliness

With the small size of glass optical fibers, dirt is a major concern. Dust particles are large compared to the core of fibers and may scratch connectors if not removed by cleaning. Patch panels have mating adapters that can become contaminated by dust if left open to the air. Test equipment has fiber-bulkhead outputs that need periodic cleaning, since they may have hundreds of insertions of test cables. Always keep dust caps on connectors, bulkhead splices, patch panels or anything else that is going to have a connection made with it. Not only will it prevent additional dust buildup, but it will prevent contamination from being touched or damaged from dropping. Always clean connectors before insertion, whether testing or connecting patchcords and equipment.

Further Study
Review the premises cabling topics on the FOA Online Reference Guide at www.foaguide.org

Review Questions

Multiple Choice
Identify the choice that best completes the statement or answers the question.

_____1.   Prior to cable plant acceptance or system turn-up, standards require that a(n) _____ is used to test the cable plant to ensure it is within the loss budget.
A. Power meter
B. LSPM or OLTS (Light source and power meter, optical loss test set)
C. OTDR
D. All of the above

_____2.   In an industrial environment, fiber is most often used to_____.
            A. Immunity to electrical noise prevents interference
            B. Provide ultra-high speed connections to machines
            C. Withstand high temperatures
            D. Tolerate physical abuse

_____3.   Which of the following are not necessary in a centralized fiber
            optic cabling architecture per industry standards?
            A. Repeaters or hubs
            B. Telecom closets
            C. Wall outlets
            D. NIC cards

_____4.   An older fiber design with a 50/125 micron core is now being
            used in cabling systems because it_____.
            A. Can be cabled in more compact cable designs
            B. Costs half as much as other multimode fibers
            C. Has a higher bandwidth with laser sources which gives more
                distance capability with gigabit (and above) networks
            D. Excess supplies are currently available from the far east

_____5.   In an multimode optical fiber, light signals travel in the
            _____ of the fiber.
            A. Core
            B. Cladding
            C. Both the core and cladding
            D. Jacket

_____6.   Which cable is used in most outdoor applications?
            A. Simplex
            B. Distribution
            C. Breakout
            D. Loose Tube

_____7.   Which connector was chosen as the standard for the most recent
            EIA/TIA 568 cabling standard?
            A. SC
            B. ST
            C. LC
            D. Any connector with a FOCIS document

_____8.   Joining of two cables in a premises cable plant run is almost always done by _____.
A. Mechanical splicing
B. Fusion splicing
C. Field installation of connectors
D. Splicing on pigtailled connectors

_____9.   Which multimode insertion loss test reference method is required in industry standards?
A. OFSTP-14
B. FOTP-34
C. FOTP-171
D. Any method as long as it is documented

_____10.   For testing a terminated fiber optic cable or a patchcord, the instrument(s) you need is (are):
A. FO power meter and light source or OLTS (optical loss test set)
B. Visual Fault Locator
C. Optical Continuous Wave Reflectometer
D. Optical Time Domain Reflectometer

Matching

Identify the three basic components of an optical fiber:

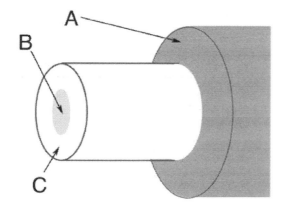

_____11.   Core

_____12.   Cladding

_____13.   Primary Buffer Coating

Additional Study and Projects

Use the FOA Online Reference Guide (www.foaguide.org) to learn more about fiber optic cable installation and termination. See how to prepare and terminate cables using the virtual hands-on (VHO) tutorials.

Learn how to install and terminate fiber optic cables in a hands-on lab. Learn how different cables are prepared and terminated using adhesive/polish and prepolished/splice termination methods.

Chapter 6
Wireless

Objectives: From this chapter you should learn:
The role of wireless in premises cabling systems
Different types of wireless systems
Why "wireless" is not "wireless"

Wireless In Structured Cabling Systems

What Is "Wireless"? Wireless uses radio frequency transmission to connect to the user - in effect replacing patchcords, allowing the final connection to be done over the radio link. Wireless allows the user to roam unencumbered by cabling within the service area covered. Examples of wireless networks are:
Cell phones
WiFi wireless networks
Bluetooth short-range wireless
WiMax broadband wireless
WiFi (IEEE 802.11) is probably most important to the typical cable installer.

No corporate network can probably be built without wireless today. People now want to be mobile. Practically everybody uses a laptop as their primary computer, excepting engineers or graphic designers at workstations, and most of them will have a laptop as a second computer to carry, along with everybody else, on trips and to meetings where everybody brings their laptops and connects on WiFi.

Besides laptops on WiFi, people use Blackberries and iPhones for wireless communications. Some new devices, like the iPhone, allow web browsing with connection over either the cellular network or a WiFi network. Some mobile phones are portable VoIP devices connecting over WiFi to make phone calls. While WiFi has had some growing pains and continual upgrades, at the IEEE 802.11n standard it has become more reliable and offers what seems to be adequate bandwidth for most users.

The desire for mobility, along with the expansion of connected services, appears to lead to a new type of corporate network. The cabling consists of a fiber optic backbone with copper to the desktop for people who want direct connections (maybe fiber to the desk for engineering or graphics users) and for everyone else, multiple wireless access points, more than is common in the past, for full coverage and maintaining a reasonable number of users per access point is the new norm for corporate networks.

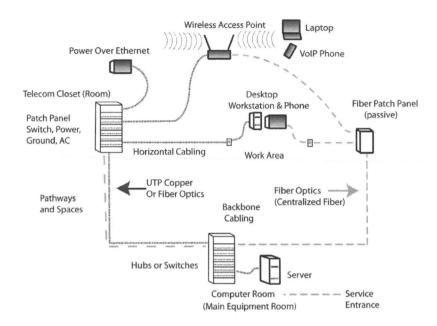

Wireless is not "wireless," as every antenna location (called an access point - AP or WAP) must be connected into the network cabling to communicate with the network electronics. The wireless connection really only replaces the patchcord that would otherwise connect the user into the network. Thus every AP must have a connection into the network, either over UTP or fiber. APs are available with either type of connection and fiber versions are not that much more expensive today.

Which wireless version should be chosen? Most premises systems use WiFi. WiFi wireless standards are developed by the IEEE 802.11 committee, and standards are under continuous upgrading. Most current networks use 802.11n which offers adequate bandwidth for most users and enough channels (frequencies) to accommodate multiple access points for good coverage. Newer, faster versions of WiFi are being developed that use mulitple frequencies and higher frequencies to increase usable bandwidth.

Wireless offers several challenges to the installer and user. First, it is important to provide good coverage in the work area. This involves installing multiple APs with overlapping coverage. Unfortunately, the coverage any AP provides depends on the environment, as objects like walls, office partitions, desks and even people absorb or reflect signals, affecting coverage.

Manufacturers' diagrams often look like the figure below with coverage a nice circle, while actual coverage looks more like the blob also shown. The "n" version of WiFi uses reflections off office spaces to enhance it's performance, so deciding where to site access points often requires a knowledgeable wireless tech scanning the office using sophisticated test gear.

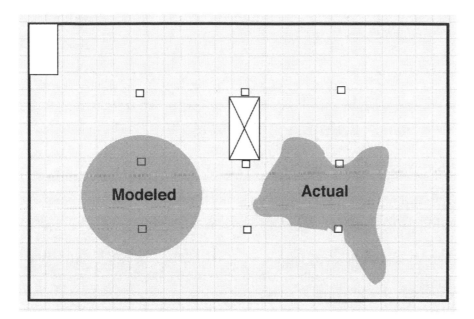

Security is the next -and perhaps biggest- problem for wireless. Any AP is a potential security flaw for those wishing to breach your network. Any company's connection to the Internet will have a firewall to prevent unauthorized entry by those outside the network, but any access point offers easy access, even to someone sitting in a car outside on the street. Securing wireless networks requires connecting them not to just any switch in the network, but to wireless controllers that filter any traffic from the AP to authorize users and monitor traffic. Controllers can also provide guest access, for example allowing guests to access the Internet but preventing unauthorized access to the corporate network. Wireless controllers must also be able to identify unauthorized APs plugged into the network, as employees are known to have done, as they are likely to be insecure.

Wireless Standards

WiFi (IEEE 802.11)
Wi-Fi (Wireless Fidelity) allows you to connect to the Internet from your couch at home, in restaurants, airports, hotel rooms or a conference room at work without wires. Wi-Fi is a wireless technology like a cell phone, but optimized for data and Internet connections. Wi-Fi enabled computers send and receive

data anywhere within the range of a base station (access point.)

WiFi was originally referring only to IEEE 802.11b version of the wireless standard, but to reduce confusion, it was expanded to include all versions of 802.11.

WiFi is the version of wireless networks most users are familiar with. Most laptops now support WiFi connections and many offices already have installed access points. It is also the version most likely to be installed by premises cabling contractors, but metropolitan networks built using WiFi will primarily be outside plant installations connecting over singlemode fiber.

There are several versions of 802.11, however, not all are compatible:

802.11: applies to wireless LANs and provides 1 or 2 Mbps transmission in the 2.4 GHz band using either frequency hopping spread spectrum (FHSS) or direct sequence spread spectrum (DSSS). 802.11 is effectively obsolete.

802.11a: an extension to 802.11 that applies to wireless LANs and provides up to 54 Mbps in the 5GHz band. 802.11a uses an orthogonal frequency division multiplexing encoding scheme rather than FHSS or DSSS.

802.11b (also referred to as 802.11 High Rate or Wi-Fi): an extension to 802.11 that applies to wireless LANS and provides 11 Mbps transmission (with a fallback to 5.5, 2 and 1 Mbps) in the 2.4 GHz band. 802.11b uses only DSSS. 802.11b was a 1999 ratification to the original 802.11 standard, allowing wireless functionality comparable to Ethernet.

802.11g: applies to wireless LANs and provides 20+ Mbps in the 2.4 GHz band.

802.11n: uses multiple channels and frequencies to transmit data at higher rates while still offering compatibility to previous 802.11 versions.

Bluetooth (IEEE 802.15)

Bluetooth is a limited distance network for consumer devices. It has been used to connect a wireless printer or mouse to a PC, wireless headsets to cell phones and stereos, cell phones to cars for hands-free operation, digital cameras to printers, etc. 802.15 is a communications specification that was approved in early 2002 by the Institute of Electrical and Electronics Engineers Standards Association (IEEE) for wireless personal area networks (WPANs). The initial version, 802.15.1, was adapted from the Bluetooth specification and is fully compatible with Bluetooth 1.1.

In terms of installation, Bluetooth is built-in to many devices and plugged into USB ports or added as cards to PCs, not installed as access points like WiFi, so it is not generally of interest for cabling installers.

WIMAX (IEEE 802.16)

WiMAX is a further development of wireless network technology that expands the data capacity of wireless to ~ 100 Mb/s and it's distance capability to several miles. WiMAX is still in the development stage, where WiFi is well established. Unlike WiFi which was primarily a short distance network aimed at private networks, WiMAX appears aimed at communications carriers who could use it in place of landline networks, substituting WiMAX, for example, for Fiber To The Home, in areas needing upgrades of their networks or using it to allow notebook PC or PDA roaming in a metropolitan area.

Like all networks, WiMAX needs a lot of standards work, here under the IEEE 802.16 committee. Products are already available, but many users are awaiting final standards and interoperability before committing to the technology. WiMAX networks will look more like cellular networks, built into the local geography like cellular phone infrastructure, requiring negotiating frequency allocations and antenna locations.

WiMAX installations will primarily be outside plant installations connecting over singlemode fiber.

Cellular Phone Networks

Cellular phone networks are the largest wireless networks with billions of users worldwide. Every day, more of those users are accessing data services using smart phones or PCs with wireless adapters. These networks are outside plant networks and beyond the scope of this web page, except as installed in large buildings like convention centers or tunnels where cellular services would not be otherwise available. These networks generally use singlemode optical fiber to connect lower power cellular antennas indoors.

Is All Wireless Really Wireless?

Wireless is only wireless to the final user, since radio spectrum is scarce and far too valuable to use for connecting antennas or access points. Cell phone towers you see everywhere are generally connected on fiber optics to the rest of the phone network - which is also fiber optics. The exception is when the towers are located in rugged terrain, where antennas provide radio relay. WiFi access points are part of structured cabling, tied into the same Ethernet network as any other Ethernet device. Convention centers and other large buildings where cell phone coverage may be spotty often use cabled antennas inside the facility to provide higher quality connections.

WiFi Access Point Requirements

Networks need Wi-Fi access points or gateways to serve as the central base station for the network. A typical Wi-Fi access point can support some 15 to 20 users, so most homes and small offices need only a single access point. However, if you have a very large dwelling (or house) or if your office is spread out, you may need more. A basic rule of thumb is 100 to 300 feet indoors and 2000 feet outdoors. Your range may vary, based on the building or environment you're using it in.

Of course, the number of access points depends on how the network is

used and the total number of users, as well as how big a space needs to be covered. A single access point can easily handle from 10 to 30 users who only use the network to send e-mail, cruise the Internet and occasionally save and retrieve large files. Within a typical office environment, most access points can provide good wireless coverage up to 150 feet or so. For large facilities with many users, or with users who require a lot of bandwidth, you may need more than a single access point. Many access points can be connected to each other wirelessly or via Ethernet cables to create a single large network. With Wi-Fi, speed decreases the farther the user is from the base station. For example, close to the base station, a "g" Wi-Fi computer should be able to get the full 11 Mbps data rate. Move farther away, and depending on environment, the data rate may drop to 1 Mbps. 1 Mbps throughput is still a perfectly acceptable performance level, if you're sending and receiving e-mail, cruising the Internet or just performing data entry tasks from a mobile computer.
An access point looks like zone cabling, in that is it is connected to the network with cable and flexibly allows connections to end users.

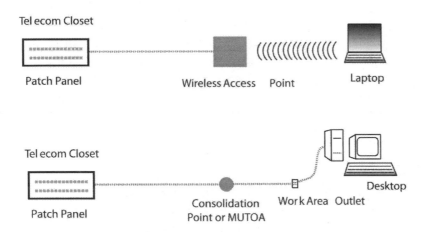

Zone Cabling: Instead of horizontal wiring going directly to the work area, terminate multiple horizontal cables at a multi-user telecommunications outlet assembly (MUTOA). MUTOAs may be located above the ceiling or or a common wall or partition. It's an ideal solution for open offices. Generally serves fewer than 12 connections. Short patchcords to work area provide user connections. Zone cabling makes networks easier and less expensive for MACs (moves, adds and changes).
The wireless access point is connected to the network on cabling (UTP or fiber) The access point may be mounted in many locations, but locations should be chosen for best range, e.g. ceiling, wall, on modular furniture or a desktop.

Wireless Design

Wireless design requires a comprehensive review of customer premises and needs. Vendors can provide much useful information on the design process. The TIA TR-42 committee that writes structured cabling standards has written TSB-162 with guidelines for designing cabling for access points.

The designer (and installer) of wireless networks needs to consider all these factors:

Coverage
Define area where wireless connectivity is desired:
Is it indoors or outdoors?
Do you need isolated areas? That is, should wireless coverage be limited to certain areas?
You need to study manufacturers specifications for antenna coverage and plan for about 30% cell overlap

Capacity
How many users should the network accomodate? While most agree a single access point can handle 10-30 users,
some vendors recommend no more than 6 users to reduce traffic slowdowns.
What types of equipment are they using? Laptops, desktop computers, PDAs, VoIP phones?
What kinds of applications? If it's mostly email and some Internet access, the data transfers will be much lower than if it is to be used for transferring large files like watching videos.
Trade off range for data rates. More access points close together will provide greater data rates, at a higher cost.

Interference
Wireless, operating in the radio spectrum, is susceptible to interference. Potential causes of interference include:
Other equipment can radiate emissions that interfere with wireless or it may be susceptible to interference from wireless, potentially critical in some applications like hospitals. Sources of interference include common items like garage door openers or other remote controls.
Other wireless networks like Bluetooth or even garage door openers that operate on similar frequencies can cause problems. In some cases, access points with overlapping coverage can cause problems, but this can be solved by setting adjacent access points to alternating channels.
Building features like metal structural beam or doors can absorb or reflect wireless signals causing problems.
Moving vehicles outdoors may reflect signals randomly causing problems

outdoors. Siting antennas high can overcome this problem.
Antenna directivity (directional or omnidirectional) can help in gaining proper coverage without interference.

Connectivity

What are network constraints? Will it be only data or is VoIP involved?
Can current network handle additional traffic or will it need upgrading?
Where will access points be cabled to? Is there space in the telecom closet?
How will additional cabling be installed? Does conduit or cable trays need to be installed also?

Security

Security is the #1 problem with wireless networks. If a wireless router is added to a network that has a direct connection to the corporate servers, it provides a convenient entry point for hackers, and password protection is inadequate - it can be cracked!
It's interesting to note that T-Mobile, the suppier of WiFi networks in many bookstores and cafes, says on their tech support website that wireless is "inherently insecure." Companies have learned that wireless access should be separate from the corporate network, usually limited to Internet access. This is adequate for company visitors and employees can access the company servers through a Internet virtual private network (VPN.)
Special wireless routers are available and they should be on separate backbones from wired outlets.

Power Requirements

The access point needs power, which can be supplied from AC power or PoE (power over Ethernet - see below.) If AC power is used, it must be installed with proper grounding and UPS backup.

Power over Ethernet

The Power over Ethernet standard from the IEEE (802.3af) allows using network UTP cabling to send power over UTP conductors to power remote devices that need power to operate, such as WiFi wireless access points, VoIP phones, surveillance cameras, hubs or switches without local power access.
Power supplies located in wiring closets (midspan devices) may provide power to cabling or Ethernet switches may be designed to supply power over the cable to compatible devices (endspan devices). It is part of the IEEE Ethernet standard (802.3af), developed with the cabling system manufacturers and is considered in cabling standards.
It is relatively low power: ~13W @ 48V, but adequate for most of the classes of devices considered like "802.11b" and "802.11g" WiFi. It's being upgraded in 802.3at to 25W but may still be inadequate for "802.11n" access points.

Site Survey - Key To Success

The most important task when installing a wireless network comes long
before any installation begins. A thorough site survey is needed to determine
how to install the best network. A site survey should be done with a survey
tool that allows scanning the
site with actual transmitters that can:
Measure performance between access points
Identify sources of interference
Determine access point locations

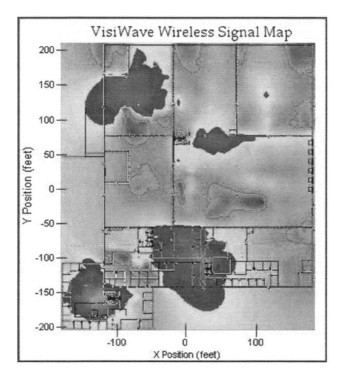

With wireless systems, it's very hard to predict network performance without
the use of the proper test equipment. Testers will give you a visual picture of
the site to help understand where access points should be placed. (Visiwave
shown) The complexity of a site survey will be determined by the size of the
network and the of the site. A good site survey will make the installation
easier and the quality of network service much better.

Further Study
Review the premises cabling topics on the FOA Online Reference Guide
at www.foaguide.org
Review Questions

True/False
Indicate whether the statement is true or false.

_____1.   The single most important part of a wireless installation is proper placement of access points to insure proper coverage.

_____2.   Practically anyone with a laptop and wireless card can access any wireless network unless security is carefully programmed.

Multiple Choice
Identify the choice that best completes the statement or answers the question.

_____3.   Wireless networks are really used to replace _____.
A. The patchcord that connects a PC to a wall outlet connection
B. Backbone cabling
C. Structured cabling
D. Routers

_____4.   The common IEEE 802.11b wireless LAN is also called
A. Bluetooth
B. WiFi
C. WiMax
D. Hot Spot

_____5.   A wireless antenna is also known as a _____.
A. Hot spot
B. Wireless router
C. WC (wireless cell)
D. Access point

_____6.   Most wireless antennas connect to the Internet by _____.
A. RF wireless
B. RG-59 Coax
C. Structured cabling (Cat 5e or fiber)
D. STP cabling

_____7.   IEEE 802.11b has a range of ____ feet.
A. 33
B. 150
C. 300
D. 1000

_____8.   Before beginning a wireless installation, it is most important that you _____.

       A. Decide which vendors to use
       B. Make sure the vendors, products work together
       C. Carefully estimate costs
       D. Do a thorough site survey

_____9.   Wireless access points can use _____ to simplify powering the equipment.
       A. Low voltage power supplies
       B. AC
       C. Power over Ethernet (IEEE 802.3ah or at)
       D. Data signal power

_____10.   Potential sources of interference for wireless LANs include

_____.
       A. Other wireless networks
       B. Remote controls like door openers
       C. Moving objects
       D. All of the above

Additional Study and Projects

Using manufacturers' data, determine the cable types for wireless access points and how the access points must be powered. See what information is available on how to locate access points for best coverage.

Chapter 7
Designing Premises Cabling Systems

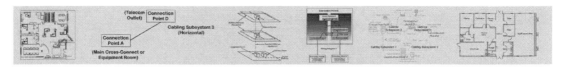

Objectives: From this chapter you should learn:
How to choose the types of cabling needed
Designing cabling as part of a building infrastructure
Creating pathways and spaces to accommodate cabling
How to document a cabling installation

The model for premises cabling standards was AT&T's design guidelines for telephone cabling and PBXes. The AT&T survey determined that 99.9% of all stations were less than 300 feet (about 100 meters) from the wiring closet, so that became the structured cabling standard. Much of the terminology from the telephone industry also carried over into the development of structured cabling standards. Over time cabling standards evolved to include fiber optic cables in the backbone and even to the desktop, allowing greater cable lengths but still following the same basic guidelines. A newer architecture, based on fiber to the home networks is becoming widespread and is described in Appendix B. This chapter will focus on traditional structured cabling.

The communications connection to the outside world comes into the building through what is called a "service entrance" and is terminated in the main "equipment room" or "main cross connect" which houses the electronic communications equipment which connects to the outside world. There may be other equipment rooms which also contain electronics located in the building connected using what is called "backbone cable."

The "telecommunications closet," or as it is now called "telecommunications room (TR)," is the (typically) small equipment room closest to the end user, where the termination of the backbone cabling and connection to "horizontal cabling" which runs to the end user occurs. It will be located in proximity to the end users, officially known as the "work area" but often called the "desktop". These locations are where all switches, hubs and any other networking equipment will be located. All cabling is defined by the necessity to connect all these locations and the desktop of the end user, which is called the "work area". The facilities in which cables are run are referred to as "pathways and spaces."

TIA-568-C revision proposes to change the nomenclature of structured cabling systems. Appendix B is an explanation of the proposal.

All equipment rooms require uninterruptible conditioned power, a separate data ground, air conditioning and an adequate amount of floor space. Proper designers and installers of these systems should be consulted if the cabling designer is not familiar with or licensed for this work.

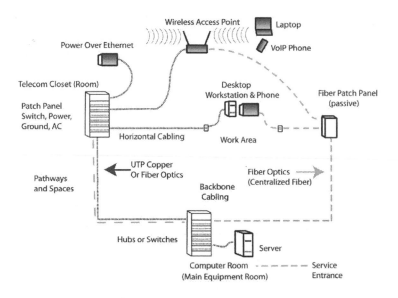

The backbone cabling can be either UTP or fiber optics. In larger networks today, fiber is most often used for its longer distance capability and higher bandwidth. 568 specifies two multimode fibers, 62.5/125 (OM1) - the most common MM fiber until network speeds exceeded 1 Gb/s, and 50/125 (OM2, OM3 or OM4 - laser optimized) - a higher bandwidth fiber compatible with all fiber equipment. OM3 50/125 fiber is rated for use with lasers for >gigabit networks and is more often the choice now. OM4 is aimed at networks operating at 10 Gb/s and higher. Singlemode fiber is also specified for longer backbone links, as in a campus, for very high speed networks or where distance exceeds even OM3 or OM4 fiber capability.

Horizontal connections have traditionally been UTP copper, compatible the network port provided on practically every type of computer gear. With the advent of wireless communications of adequate bandwidth and the inclusion of wireless adapters in all laptops and many other portable devices, wireless has become the user connection of choice.

Virtually every corporate network now includes wireless, which is, of course, not wireless, since access points are connected into the network with copper or fiber cabling. Provision is necessary in the design of a facility for adequate numbers of access points, cabling to the access points and proper power, also conditioned and uninterruptible.

Fiber optics is also a horizontal option in 568, but not often used because of the higher cost of electronics. The exception is where high bitrate networks or future upgrades are expected. However, a properly designed centralized fiber network that connects the desktop directly to the computer room with no intermediate electronics, only passive interconnections, does not need a telecom room and saves the cost of conditioned power, data ground, AC and the floor space of the telecom room, which may offset the additional cost of the fiber electronics.

The telecom closet, or telecom room (TR) as it is now called, houses the hubs for the computers in the work areas. These hubs are interconnected on "backbone" wiring which is mostly fiber optics, as it usually carries higher speed signals over longer distances and provides isolation from ground loops, another problem with copper cabling in LANs. The main cross-connect (MXC) or equipment room contains the network and telco hardware. For traditional POTS (plain old telephone service) telephones, their lower bandwidth requirements allow longer runs, so they are usually simply connected to backbone cables in the telecom room with a punchdown and run straight to the PBX. Many users are now using VoIP (voice over Internet protocol) phones which share network cables with LANs.

Cabling Design Criteria

Cable Types
Cabling for premises networks has many options, mostly determined by performance of the cabling. Today, one can choose UTP cabling of grades, called categories, commonly referred to as Cat 5 (Category 5), Cat 5e (enhanced Category 5), Cat 6 and Cat 6A (augmented Category 6). Higher ratings are for cables with higher bandwidth and other performance specifications, explained here. Likewise, fiber is rated as OM1, OM2, OM3 and some called OM3+ by manufacturers until OM4 standards were ratified. Again, higher ratings are for fiber with higher bandwidth capability., explained here.

As you might expect higher performance cable supports higher bit rate systems, and in the case of fiber, longer link distances (copper is limited by the standards and the laws of physics) but at a higher cost. Users generally choose the highest bandwidth cabling they can justify as it provides more "headroom" for networks installed today and more likelihood of supporting faster networks in the future.

A general restriction for structured cabling is the permissible distances for cable runs. The table below lists cable distances for various types of permitted cabling. The restrictions on fiber links in the horizontal are arbitrary to be equal to copper cabling and may be exceeded for many network uses. Fiber lengths in the backbone may be restricted by the bandwidth of the fiber when used with high speed networks.

Cable Distances

Cable Type	Distance (M)	Distance (F)
UTP copper (data)	100	330
UTP copper (voice-POTS)	800	2625
MM fiber (horizontal)	100	330
MM fiber (centralized)	300	1000
MM fiber (backbone)	2000	6560
SM fiber (backbone)	3000	9840

Copper cabling designed into a network is allowed 100 meters total length, comprised of 90m of permanently installed cable (the "permanent link") and up to 10m of patchcords used to interconnect cabling or connect active networking equipment. As long as the installed length does not exceed 90m, it meets the standards, and, if properly installed, should pass certification tests.

Fiber has much more leeway in premises cabling, with longer lengths possible and more options in termination. When designing fiber networks, one must design the paths for the installed cables, estimate the lengths and do an analysis of the losses incurred in that section, called a loss budget, to determine if the link will meet the standards and support the network electronics proposed as well as create pass/fail criteria for testing.

All premises cables, copper or fiber, must be rated per electrical codes for flammability in order to be used indoors. Copper cables are rated differently than fiber, which may be non-conductive or conductive if metallic elements are included in the cable design. Refer to the cable sections for more detail on cable ratings.

Designing Pathways and Spaces
Industry standards cover designing pathways and spaces in great detail. Certainly providing adequate space and proper design of cabling systems is needed for a correct installation. However, the design of pathways and spaces is hardly the sole responsibility of the cabling designer, contractor or installer. It is a cooperative effort that should involve a the owner and/or lessor of the facility, the architects and engineers, information technology personnel and other contractors: mechanical, electrical, plumbing, etc. Familiarity of the needs of cabling and industry standards is important to all these parties in order to complete a successful installation.

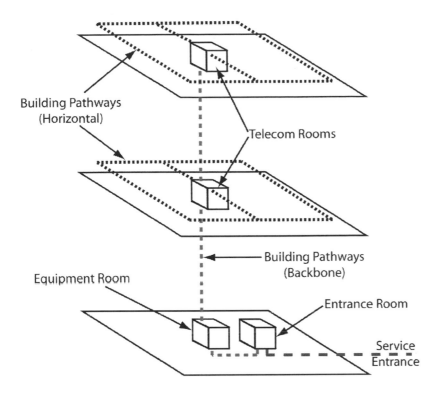

Proper installation depends on proper design. The facility in which cabling is being installed should be designed according to industry standards which include all the pathways and spaces in which cabling and equipment will be installed. Even where the cables are routed in the building is important. Cables need to be kept dry and in moderate temperatures. Above the ceiling in some buildings in hot climates can get very hot, causing UTP cable to have higher attenuation so it will not support full standard link distances. Supports for the cables should be wide enough to support the cables without distortion, spaced close enough so the weight of cable supported (copper cable bundles are heavy!) and have no sharp edges to cut or kink the cables.

The performance of the cabling network is also heavily dependent on the installation. The components used in structured cabling installation have been carefully designed and exhaustively tested to meet or exceed the requirements of EIA/TIA 568 for performance at 100-250 MHz. If the cabling is not properly designed and installed, performance will be degraded.

Pathways & Spaces

Horizontal pathways are facilities for the installation of telecommunications cable from the telecommunications closet to the work area telecommunications outlet/connector.

Backbone pathways consist of intra- and interbuilding pathways that provide the means for placing backbone cables between the entrance room or space, telecommunications closets, equipment rooms, or the main terminal space. Backbone pathways may be either vertical or horizontal depending on the building layout. Interbuilding backbone pathways extend between buildings. Intrabuilding backbone pathways are contained within a building. Pathways encompass underfloor, access floor, conduit, tray and wireway, ceiling, and perimeter facilities. The pathway and cable type will determine the maximum number of cables that can be accomodated and vice versa. The design shall provide a suitable means and method for supporting cables from equipement room to the telecommunications closet (backbone) and from the telecommunications closet to the work areas to be served (horizontal.) Cable shall not be laid directly on the ceiling tile or rails. All pathways shall be installed, grounded and bonded per applicable building, fire and electrical codes.

Work Areas

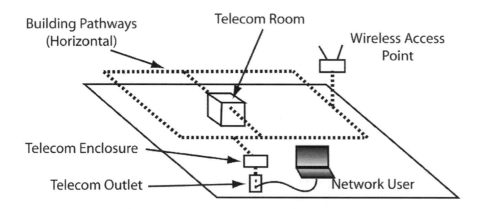

A work area is where a user is sited. The work area my be an office or area divided by modular office furniture. For planning purposes, a user should be allocated approximately 10 m2 or 100 square feet of floor space. Each work area should have at least one cabling outlet with one voice and one data jack. This outlet should be placed within 1 m (3 ft) of a power outlet.
Work areas may be divided into zones encompassing several work areas which are served by multi-user telecom outlet assemblies (MUTOA) mounted on building walls or columns (not above ceilings) and use short drop cables to each user.

Telecommunications Room (Closet)
The telecommunications room on each floor is the location of the common access point for backbone and horizontal pathways. The telecommunications closet is designed to contain telecommunications equipment, cable terminations, and associated cross-connect cable/wiring.

The telecommunications closet shall be located as close as practicable to the center of the area served. Telecom rooms should not share space with other facilities including electrical with the exception of electrical services required for the equipment placed in the room.

There should be one telecom room per floor or more where the areas served are greater than 1000 m2 or 10,000 ft2 or the distance to work areas will exceed 90m, the maximum length of permanently installed cable.

Telecom room space should be large enough for the served area. In new buildings, requirements should be coordinated with the architect and mechanical contractors. In existing structures, rooms may need to be constructed.

Telecom Room Floor Area

Served Area	(Floor Space)	Room Size	(Dimensions)
m2	ft2	m	ft
1000	10,000	3 X 3.4	10 X 11
800	8,000	3 X 2.8	10 X 9
500	5,000	3 X 2.2	10 X 7

Traditionally, telecom rooms have had two walls covered by 20 mm (3/4 in) plywood to support attached equipment, including large arrays of punchdown blocks for POTS cables. With the widespread usage of racks of patch panels, such may not be needed and should be decided with the cooperation of the user.

Telecom rooms need conditioned, uninterruptible power and a data ground. Lighting and other electrical equipment should be run off the normal building power. Adequate AC must be provided to maintain the temperature the same as the surrounding area or at least within the operating limits of the equipment.

Equipment Room

The equipment room is a centralized space for telecommunications equipment (e.g., PBX, computing equipment, servers, switches, routers, storage devices, video switches, etc. that serve occupants of the facility). Any or all of the functions of a telecommunications closet or entrance facility may alternately be provided by an equipment room. The equipment room should be restricted to telecom equipment and adequate security provided.

The room should be sized for current and future usage. Guidelines for floor area of the equipment room are given in the table below. Accessibility for large equipment is often necessary and should be provided.

Equipment Room Floor Area

# Work Areas	Room Area (m2)	Room Area (ft2)
<100	14	150
101-400	37	400
401-800	74	800
801-1200	111	1200

Like telecom rooms, the equipment room needs conditioned, uninterruptible power and a data ground. Lighting and other electrical equipment should be run off the normal building power. Adequate AC must be provided to maintain the temperature the same as the surrounding area or at least within the operating limits of the equipment.

Entrance Facility

The entrance facility consists of the telecommunications service entrance to the building, including the entrance through the building wall, and continuing to the entrance room or space. The entrance facility may contain the backbone pathways that link to the main terminal space and to other buildings in campus situations. Antenna entrances may also constitute part of the entrance facility.

All carriers and telecommunications providers involved in providing service to the building shall be contacted to establish their requirements and explore alternatives for delivering service. The location of other utilities, such as electrical, water, gas, and sewer, shall be considered in the selection of the telecommunications entrance facility location. A service entrance pathway shall be provided, The basic methods for provisioning are underground, buried, aerial pathways, and tunnels. Some facilities also will require wireless connections from satellite or digital radio links. The location of that facility and its connections to the entrance facility need to be considered in the design phase.

The entrance room or space is the component of the entrance facility that provides space for the placing and termination of protectors on the entrance cable and may contain network interface devices. If network interface devices and telecommunications equipment are required in the entrance room, additional space will be needed.

Other Design Considerations

Numerous issues must be addressed in the construction of a cabling system, many of which involve other parties (e.g. the end user, IT personnel, architects, engineers, electricians and other contractors). Cabling pathways and spaces must maintain separation from electrical conductors per electrical codes, provide protection from lightning and other power surges, be protected from electromagnetic interference (EMI) and be properly grounded and bonded. All penetrations must be properly firestopped per building codes.

Documentation

One cannot emphasize strongly enough the value of documentation. Documentation should be part of the design process, creating the nomenclature and database used throughout the installation process. Installation should be done according to the documentation created in design and every cable, patch panel or other equipment marked properly. TIA 606 is the US standard for cable plant administration which includes marking and documentation. Nothing facilitates proper installation, testing, upgrades, moves/adds/changes or restoration more than proper documentation.

Further Study
Review the premises cabling topics on the FOA Online Reference Guide at www.foaguide.org

Review Questions

Multiple Choice
Identify the choice that best completes the statement or answers the question.

_____1.   Structured cabling standards call for a maximum length of UTP
         cable for data of _____.
         A. 90 meters
         B. 100 meters
         C. 300 meters
         D. 800 meters

_____2.   Structured cabling standards allow for a maximum length of
         permanently installed (not including patchcords) UTP cable for
         data of _____.
         A. 90 meters
         B. 100 meters
         C. 300 meters
         D. 800 meters

_____3.   UTP cable installed above the ceiling can _____ the
         ceiling tiles.
         A. not be laid on
         B. be hung from frames of
         C. be laid directly on top of
         D. must be sleeved to be laid on top of

_____4.   UTP cable installed above the ceiling in hot climates may not
         _____.
         A. Meet crosstalk specs
         B. Pass certification tests
         C. Be fire safe
         D. Support full standard link distances

_____5.   Structured cabling standards call for a maximum length of UTP
         cable for voice (POTS) of _____.
         A. 90 meters
         B. 100 meters
         C. 300 meters
         D. 800 meters

_____6.   Structured cabling standards call for a maximum length of
singlemode fiber optic cable for backbones of _____.
A. 800 meters
B. 1000 meters
C. 3000 meters
D. 2000 meters

_____7.   Structured cabling standards call for a maximum length of
multimode fiber optic cable for backbones of _____.
A. 800 meters
B. 1000 meters
C. 3000 meters
D. 2000 meters

_____8.   For planning office layout, each user should be allocated _____
floor space.
A. Adequate
B. 100 sq ft
C. 3 sq m
D. shared

_____9.   Each floor should be allocated one _____ when floor space is
under 10,000 sq ft.
A. Equipment room
B. MUTOA
C. User
D. Telcom room (closet)

_____10.   Both equipment rooms and telecom rooms should have

_____.
A. Uninterruptible power
B. Air conditioning
C. Data quality ground
D. All of the above

_____11.   One cannot emphasize strongly enough the value of _____.
A. Standards
B. Cabling
C. Fiber optics
D. Documentation

Additional Study and Projects

Review manufacturers' literature on designing cabling systems to TIA structured cabling standards. For a building, hypothetical or real, design a cabling system, specifying backbone and horizontal cabling types for medium (1 Gb/s) and high speed (10 Gb/s) backbones, copper in the horizontal, centralized fiber and wireless coverage.

Chapter 8
Premises Cabling Installation

Objectives: From this chapter you should learn:
What is involved in a premises cabling installation
The role of the contractor and installer
How to prepare for the installation
Proper installation techniques for premises cabling
Safety in cabling installation
Removing and recycling abandoned cabling

After the process of designing a premises cabling network is completed, the next step is to install it. What do we mean by the "installation process?" Assuming the design is completed, we're looking at the process of physically installing and completing the network, turning the design into an operating system.

Preparing For Installation

The Role of the Contractor in an Installation
To begin work on a premises cabling installation, the network owner or user must choose a contractor, perhaps the most important decision in the entire process. The contractor should be able to work with the customer in each installation project through six stages: design, installation, testing, troubleshooting, documentation and restoration. The contractor must be experienced in premises cabling installations of the type involved and should be able to provide references for similar work.
One should be able to rely the contractor to not only do the installation but to assist in the design of the network and help choose components and vendors. Once the contractor has been given the assignment, they should be able to help the customer with the design, including choosing the right kinds of cables, connectors and hardware for the installation. The contractor should know which components meet industry standards to ensure interoperability and what state of the art components will facilitate future expandability.
The experienced contractor also should be able to help in the choice of vendors. Experience with particular product types and vendors will allow the contractor to assist the customer to choose products that make the installation

faster and easier as well as higher performance and more reliable. Should the customer choose components that are unfamiliar to the contractor, it is important that the contractor know early in the process so they may obtain proper training, often from the manufacturer, as well as any unique tools that may be required.

Generally, the customer is not as familiar with premises cabling technology and practice as an experienced contractor. The contractor may need to discuss certain choices with the customer where they believe alternatives may be better choices.

The actual installation process can involve more than just putting in cable, terminating and testing it. If the contractor is knowledgeable and experienced, the user may ask the contractor to purchase, receive, inspect and bring components to the work site also, which can be another good source of revenue for the contractor. Having full control of the materials process can also make life easier for the contractor, as they have a better chance to keep on schedule rather than depending on a customer who has many other priorities. Plus, they may have the latitude to choose components they are more familiar with, facilitating the actual installation process.

The technicians actually doing the installation should be trained and certified by organizations like The FOA (www.thefoa.org) which offers the CPCT premises cabling technician certification and/or manufacturers of the products being installed. Certification provides a level of confidence that the installation techs are knowledgeable and have the skills needed for the work involved.

The final four requirements from the contractor, testing, troubleshooting, documentation and restoration, need to be discussed before the project ever begins. Every premises cabling project requires loss testing of every link according to industry standards. The contractor and customer must agree that testing includes troubleshooting problems and fixing them as well as documenting test results for every link.

Likewise, for the contractor, documentation must begin before the project starts so the scope of work is known to everyone and end only when the final test data is entered. Copies of the documentation, along with excess components left over from the installation, must be presented to the customer to facilitate future network restoration, should it be required.

The Contract

The contract for a premises cabling installation should include detailed requirements for the project, spelling out exactly what is to be installed, acceptable test results, and documentation to be provided. All this should be discussed between the customer and the contractor and agreed to in writing. They are not irrelevant details, as they are important to ensure the customer gets what they expect and the contractor knows what is expected of them when designing the network, estimating costs, doing the actual installation and providing proof of performance in order to show the work is completed and payment should be made.

Planning For The Project

Once the contracts are signed and a set of plans has been handed to the contractor, what's next? Planning the job is the first task. Proper planning is important to ensure the job is installed properly, on time and meets cost objectives, so the contractor can make a profit.

It is assumed you have a finished design for the project, know where and how everything will be installed and have any special requirements like permits ready. One can also assume you have a completion date, hopefully a reasonable one, to work toward. The first step then is to create a schedule which will be the centerpiece of the planning process.

In order to schedule a job, you need a lot of information, much of which can be acquired from estimates you did when bidding the job. When buyers price the components to be used on a job, they should get delivery times as well as prices. Some items used on premises cabling projects should be stock items, like UTP cables, connectors or patch panels. Fiber optic cables, however, may have to be made to order.

Many fiber optic cables are custom items, depending on the cable type, number and types of fibers and color coding. Custom cables will often be less expensive because they don't have extra fibers for specifications you don't need, for example, but they will have longer lead times since they must be made from scratch. Whenever specifying a fiber optic cable, always try to have a few extra fibers available, just in case fibers are damaged during installation.

The astute contractor tries to always use the same types of components on every job so they are familiar with not only the installation procedures but the typical costs, yield (i.e. number of links will pass testing first time) and any problems likely to be encountered.

If any components are not familiar to the installers, they need to learn how to install them correctly, either by experimenting in the office on off-time or getting manufacturers to train them. The need for training may also arise if new equipment types are required, such as new tools or new types of test equipment. The cardinal rule of installation is never take an unfamiliar component or tool on the job; it's a recipe for disaster.

Buyers need to order the components when the job is acquired, scheduling delivery to the job site either to have everything available before the installation begins, or on a large job with an extended schedule, according to how long the installation of that component will take. Here you also need to plan on where the components will be delivered to, either a staging area in your warehouse, for example, or to the job site.

Components delivered to the job site may require security. Theft can be a problem with cable particularly, since many thieves know all cables contain copper and the price of copper is still high! But vandalism is another concern, requiring components be either locked up or if too large to put indoors like large spools of cable or innerduct, may require on site overnight guards. Next, one needs to schedule labor. Again, the estimates should tell you how many installers of what experience will be needed and how long they are expected to need to complete the installation. If any training is needed, additional time may need to be added to the schedule.

Having covered labor and materials in the schedule, the planning is almost done. Review the schedule with everyone involved to get them on board and start the processes, beginning with acquiring materials. Then add to the plan a review of safety rules for supervisors, installers and anyone expected to be on site. Also add notes to keep all scrap cable, connectors, etc. to package and present to the user in case they are needed for future restoration.

If the start date is not tomorrow (because the customer wanted it yesterday!) and you have other projects in the interim, pull out this schedule regularly to check if everything is on schedule to prevent any last minute surprises.

Installation Checklist

Planning for the installation is a critical phase of any project as it involves coordinating activities of many people and companies. The best way to keep everything straight is to develop a checklist based on the design. The checklist below is comprehensive but each project will have some of its own unique requirements that need to be added to the list.

Pre-install checklist:
* Main point of contact/project manager chosen
* Link communications requirements set
* Equipment and component requirements set and vendors chosen
* Permits obtained
* Cable plant components and vendors chosen
* Coordination with facilities and electrical personnel complete
* Documentation completed and ready for installation, preliminary restoration plans ready
* Test plan complete
* Schedule and start date set for installation, all parties notified
* Components ordered and delivery date set, plans made for receiving materials (time, place) arrange security if left outside or on construction site
* Contractor/installer chosen and start date set
* Link route tour with contractor(s)
* Construction plans reviewed with contractor(s)
* Components chosen reviewed with contractor(s)
* Schedule reviewed with contractor(s)

- Safety rules reviewed with contractor(s)
- Excess materials being kept for restoration reviewed with contractor(s)
- Test plan reviewed with contractor(s)

Before starting the install:
- All permits available for inspection
- Sites prepared, power available
- All components on site, inspected, 24-hour security arranged if necessary
- Contractor available
- Relevant personnel notified
- Safety rules posted on the job site(s) and reviewed with all supervisors and installation personnel

During The Installation:
- Inspect workmanship at every step
- Daily review of process, progress, test data
- Immediate notification and solution of problems, shortages, etc.

After completion of cable plant installation:
- Inspect workmanship
- Review test data on cable plant
- Set up and test communications system
- Update and complete documentation
- Update and complete restoration plan
- Store restoration plan, documentation, components, etc.

Preparing The Site For Premises Installations

Before beginning installation of premises cabling and hardware, the site must be properly prepared for the installation of cables, hardware and transmission equipment. During the design and planning stages, the site should have been inspected and all the hardware necessary for the cable plant included in the design.

Premises Support Structures
There are numerous structures used for the securing of cabling in premises installations making generalizations difficult. Cable may be hung on appropriate hangers, laid in cable trays above the ceiling or below the floor or pulled into conduit or innerduct. Termination of the cables can be at racks in telecom rooms, in wall-mounted boxes or even wall outlets. Preparing for an install includes planning for storage of cable service loops behind racks such as shown here.

You must install support structures for cable installations before the installation of the cable itself. These structures should follow the guidelines of appropriate standards such as TIA/EIA 569-A and NECA/BICSI 568-2001. Allow for future growth in the quantity and size of cables when determining the size of the pathways. Follow all cable bend radius requirements and avoid pulling cables around hazards if possible.

Sometimes new cables can be laid in existing cable trays. Do not install a fiber optic cable in a conduit or duct that already contains cabling, regardless of the cable type to prevent damage. Existing or new empty ductwork can be modified to accept several different installations by the proper placement of innerduct.

Premises support structures also include patch panels for terminations. They may be wall- or rack mounted and must be chosen appropriately for the cable types being used. Terminated simplex or zipcord fiber optic cables can be terminated on open panels, but 900 micron tight-buffered fibers from distribution cables require closed termination panels for protection. If possible, the design of support structures should be such that adequate space is provided for termination of the cables and storage for service loops.

Fire Stopping

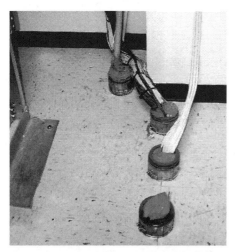

Premises cabling requires firestopping at all penetrations of walls and floors.

Telecommunications firestopping must always comply with applicable codes and standards. All penetrations should be protected by type-approved firestops.

In most areas the breaching of a fire separation will require physical monitoring until it has been repaired. Check with the "Authority Having Jurisdiction" for specific requirements on the project before commencing work.

Electrical Systems

All communications equipment will require proper power at the locations of the equipment, generally the main equipment room and telecom rooms. Power must be high quality power, protected for surges and spikes, and generally must have appropriate backup capacity to prevent loss of communications during power loss. Data equipment will require a separate ground and adequate power for year-round air conditioning. Consideration should be given to efficiency in cooling to reduce power consumption. Consult with the site owner, customer and appropriate user personnel to plan electrical power installation.

Grounding and Bonding

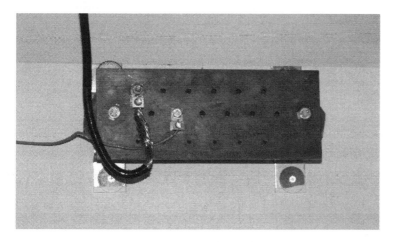

All conductive cabling and components must be grounded and bonded. Ground systems must be designed as specified by the NEC or other applicable codes and standards. Any metallic hardware used in cabling systems (such as wall-mounted termination boxes, racks, and patch panels) must be grounded. All conductive cables require proper grounding and bonding for applicable conductors.

Marking and Identifying Cables

Cables should be specified with colored jackets per industry standards which identify the cables as fiber optic cables and indicate the type of fiber in the cable. UTP terminations in patch panels should have every jack identified. All fiber optic cable terminations should be marked on racks or boxes where the cables terminate. Fiber optic cables should be tagged with identification that they are fiber optic cables and proper handling is required.

Particular care should be taken in premises cabling upgrades. For nearly two decades, 62.5/125 micron multimode fiber has been the primary fiber for premises cabling. With the emergence of gigabit networks, laser-optimized 50/125 fiber has become more popular. Mixing the two fibers can result in excessive loss at connections that may cause systems to not operate properly. Color coding, marking and even using incompatible connectors (SC or ST on 62.5/125 and LC on 50/125 fiber) should be used whenever possible.

Removal and Recycling of Abandoned Cables

Unless directed by the owner or other agency that unused cables are reserved for future use and the cables are marked accordingly, it may be required to remove abandoned optical fiber cable (cable that is not terminated at equipment other than a connector and not identified for future use with a tag) as required by the National Electrical Code or local codes.

At the discretion of the owner of the site, the contractor may be requested to remove other cables (e.g. copper communications or power cables) in addition. Removal of cables is much more time consuming than installation, as each cable must be identified and carefully removed to prevent damaging other cables. No cable should be cut for removal unless it is positively identified as one to be removed.

All cables removed should be recycled properly. Most communications cable has significant scrap value, not only for any copper conductors but for other metallic elements and even some plastics. In order to maximize your return on selling scrap cable to recyclers, there are some guidelines that should be followed.

Separate cables by type. The best price is for electrical power cable, obviously, since the copper content is higher than for communications cable, so it should be separated from other cables. Recyclers grade cable by conductor size, basically larger or smaller than 12 gage wire. Also separate communications cables by jacket type. Not only is the copper recycled, but so is the plastic. Some recycled plastics can be reused while others are processed for use as fillers or to make structures like park benches. However, the different types of jackets on riser and plenum cable, for example, require segregation for recycling.

Do not try to remove jacketing on cables. As mentioned above, the copper and plastic can both be reused. Some "scrap dealers" tell people that the cable is worth more without the jackets and they can remove it by burning it off. That's an environmental disaster, as many harmful chemicals are released into the air and may subject you to an EPA fine, plus it's dangerous. One of the largest fires ever in New York City was caused by thieves stealing wire from abandoned buildings who tried to burn off the insulation. Legitimate recyclers use two methods to remove insulation, squeezing the cable until it cuts through the insulation or chopping it into fine particles and separating metallic and plastic pieces. The chopping process works on fiber optic cable too.

Remove and separate non-cable scrap. Try to cut off connectors, cable ties, steel hangers, etc. to leave only the pure cable. Likewise, scour the job site for other recyclables, as any metallic or plastic scrap is probably recyclable. Conduit is especially good to recycle but even patchcords and extension cords are recyclable. Try to separate anything containing lead or other hazardous metals like mercury and anything considered toxic. Be aware that some electronic materials must be properly recycled according to EPA regulations. In today's world, we need to minimize the amount of material that goes to landfills because of the cost as well as the environmental impact.

Deal with legitimate recyclers. Many scrap dealers are middle-men, reselling to recyclers. Find a recycler, preferably one who owns the machinery to process cable locally, and you will get a better price and be assured the materials are properly handled. Local governments can help you find them. If you have a big enough load, they will often pick it up for you. And make certain they have a certified scale.

Installing Cabling

Cabling can be installed in many ways, under floors or above ceilings in cable trays, inside conduit, in J-hooks attached to walls or roof supports, inside walls, even inside special cable trays built into modular furniture. Installations need to be tailored to the property being cabled, the equipment being connected and local building codes, making generalizations about installations difficult. For all installations, however, certain cautions apply. Mistakes in installation of cabling, particularly UTP cable, can be detrimental to final cabling performance and very difficult to detect. A mistake that could keep the entire system from working might not show up at all until the system is completely installed and turned on.

The installer needs to remember that while cabling systems have been thoroughly researched and standardized, the standards were created as universal performance standards for the manufacturers of cabling systems. The manufacturers interpret these standards in their product development, so while components from different manufacturers are designed to be interoperable, they may not have the same installation procedures. Thus it is imperative that the installer thoroughly understand the installation procedures provided by the manufacturer for the components being installed in order to obtain the specified performance.

Start With A Good Design

Proper installation depends on the proper design of the cabling system. The facility in which cabling is being installed should be designed according to industry standards which include all the pathways and spaces in which the cabling and communications equipment will be installed. Even where the cables are routed in the building is important. Cables should be kept dry and in moderate temperatures. Above the ceiling in some buildings in hot climates can get very hot, causing UTP cable to have higher attenuation so it will not support full standard link distances.

Cable should be installed on special hooks, bridle rings or cable trays that limit its bend radius and stress to preserve the performance. You cannot lay the cable on top of ceilings or hang from the drop ceiling hangers - in most places it's illegal - not allowed by code. Supports for the cables should be wide enough to support the cables without distortion, spaced close enough so the weight of cable supported (copper cable bundles are heavy) causes minimal sagging and have no sharp edges to cut or kink the cables.   Fiber optic cables should be separated from heavy copper cables to prevent crushing; sometimes fiber cables are run in flexible orange innerduct which not only protects the cable but makes it readily visible.

Install and Terminate Cable Properly

The performance of the cabling network is also heavily dependent on the installation. The components used in structured cabling installation have been carefully designed and exhaustively tested to meet or exceed the requirements of EIA/TIA 568 or ISO 11801 when properly installed. If the cable is not properly installed, performance will be degraded. Terminations, both with UTP and fiber optic cables, must be properly made and tested.

Just like we keep reminding you about maintaining the pair twists right down to the terminations, there are other things you must realize to maintain the performance of Cat 5e/6/6a UTP cable. First of all, pulling tension must be less than 25 pounds. That's not very much tension. Pulling at higher tension can stretch the cable and affect the twists in the pairs, and it's those twists that make the cable perform well at high frequencies. Fiber optic cable can be pulled at higher tension than copper if it is properly attached to the pulling rope using only the strength members of the cable.

Pulling cable in conduit is especially critical as you must deal with friction in the conduit and pulling around bends. Installing breakout boxes for intermediate pulls is often necessary and one may need to use pulling lubricants in the conduit. Only use an appropriate lubricant to prevent long term degradation of the cable. The lubricant must be compatible with the cable jacket which can vary according to cable types and ratings. Likewise, kinking any cable by letting it get twisted or pulled around sharp corners can cause permanent damage.

One should also avoid bundling the cables too tightly. Crushing the cables can affect the performance, since it can affect the twist and pair alignment in the cable which affects high frequency performance. If one uses regular plastic cable ties, they should be tightened only finger tight and cut off - do not use cable tie guns which may tighten tight enough to damage the cables. Preferably use "hook and loop" cable ties (shown above) which have an added advantage that they can easily be opened to add or remove cables.

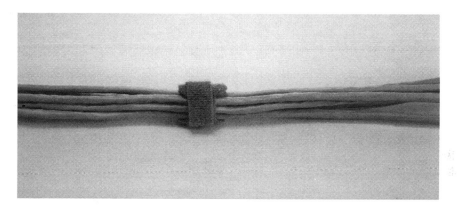

Most UTP cable shipping boxes are designed to allow easy pulling directly from the box. Gather up several boxes and pull a bunch of cables at once. Tape them together and attach a pullstring or just feed them along by hand. There is usually 1,000 feet (about 300 meters) of cable in each box. Each cable is also marked with a distance every few feet so you can keep track of length by reading the distance off the cable. *Before you pull any cable from the box, find the distance marked on the cable and write it down on top of the box.* That way, you can calculate the length of each cable you pull and more importantly, the amount remaining in the box! It's not good to start pulling a cable and find out it's not long enough!

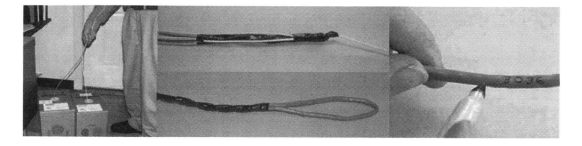

You can pull from the telecom room or to the room, whichever is more convenient in the install you are doing. You can also pull to consolidation points then out to individual outlets or vice versa, instead of pulling the bundle of cables all the way. Riser installations are more easily done by dropping cables down rather than pulling up. Riser installations need to be secured at regular intervals to prevent the weight of the cables suspended from causing long term problems.

In the telecom room, patch panels can have a large number of cables, so managing these cables can be quite a task in itself. It is important to keep all cables neatly bundled and labeled so they can be moved when necessary. However, it is also important to maintain the integrity of the cables, preventing kinking or bending in too small a radius which may adversely affect frequency performance.

Safety

Power cables can be a safety hazard. Although premises cable is called "low voltage" and fiber optic cables are non-conductive, it runs in areas full of power cables that can be a shock hazard. If you are not familiar with electrical safety, fire safety and inspections, it is strongly suggested that you take a course on the NEC (National Electric Code) or similar local codes to learn about these important topics. *It could save your life!*

Other safety considerations:

*   Become familiar with all work rules that apply to the job, including fiber codes and regulartory rules (NEC and OSHA in the US.)
*   Hard hat, safety glasses, appropriate gloves and steel toe shoes are recommended.
*   Observe ladder safety rules - many installations require work above ceilings.
*   If working in an area where other workers are present, block off your work area, especially when working above the ceiling, to protect others in the area.

Inspection

Electrical inspectors do not always inspect communications wiring. Nonetheless, take a moment to check with local electrical inspectors before you do any work in their jurisdictions. In most cases, the inspector of your installation will be the same person who signs you contract, although in some cases, the inspector will be a third party. Make sure you know who will inspect your work before you give your customer a final price. You must know what the inspector will expect of you and what he or she will be looking for.

Installation Tips

- All UTP cabling components must be equally rated at the highest level expected from the installation (e.g. all Cat5e rated for Cat 5e performance).
- UTP cable must be pulled from the reel or box without kinking.
- UTP cable must be pulled with less than 25 pounds of tension.
- Use cable lubricant in conduit if necessary, but ensure it is compatible with the cable being pulled.
- Cable must not be pulled around sharp corners or kinked.
- Inspect the cable routes for surfaces that may abrade the cable.
- On riser installations (overhead installation), try to lower the cable down, not pull up and secure carefully at recommended intervals.
- Cables must be supported to prevent stress. Cable supports should not have sharp edges that may distort the cable.
- Cable ties must not be so tight as to distort the jacket of the cable. They are only used to prevent unnecessary movement of the cable, so snug is tight enough.
- Follow manufacturers instructions for all component installations.
- Carefully follow all codes and firestop all penetrations.

Further Study
Review the premises cabling topics on the FOA Online Reference Guide at www.foaguide.org

Review Questions

True/False
Indicate whether the statement is true or false.

_____1.   Riser cables are more easily installed by dropping cables down than pulling them up.

_____2.   Power cables are a safety hazard because so many installations involve working in areas with many power cables.

_____3.   The NEC does not refer to UTP or fiber cables because they are low voltage.

_____4.   Electrical inspectors do not always inspect communications wiring.

_____5.   Cable ties must not be so tight as to distort the jacket of the cable.

Multiple Choice
Identify the choice that best completes the statement or answers the question.

_____6.   To maintain rated performance, twists in each pair must be
maintained to within _____ of the termination.
A. 1/2 inch
B. 1 inch
C. 25 mm
D. 2.5 cm

_____7.   UTP cable is designed to be pulled with no more than _____
pounds tension.
A. 5
B. 15
C. 25
D. 50

_____8.   Supports for UTP cables should be _____.
A. Mounted on walls, not ceilings
B. Wide enough to support cables without distortion
C. Able to support deep bundles of cables
D. Made of plastic for safety

_____9.   _____ should be used to bundle cables since _____.
A. Hook and loop cable ties, tight cable ties can affect cable
performance
B. Cable ties tightened with guns, cables should not be allowed
to move around
C. Cable ties, loose cables are a safety hazard
D. Rubber bands, the stretch

_____10.   Most _____ are designed to allow easy pulling.
A. Cables
B. Cable trays
C. Cable boxes
D. Ropes

_____11.   You can keep track of how much cable is left in a box if you
            _____.
            A. Record on the cable box the beginning distance marked on
                the cable
            B. Read the distance off the cable
            C. Weigh the box
            D. You can't

Additional Study and Projects
Review safety standards including OSHA or the local equivalent that apply to premises cabling installations. Visit actual installations to see how they were implemented. In labs or an actual facility, participate in the installation of a cable plant.

Appendix A
KSAs for CPCT

The ability to perform any job requires certain abilities, knowledge and skills, commonly referred to as "KSAs." For the premises cabling technician, these KSAs have been determined from over 30 years of experience in actual installations. The FOA has developed this list to provide training organizations and instructors a list of topics that should be included in a basic training curriculum, as for CPCT certification. For those working in the field who wish to become CPCT certified, it is a list of relevant topics for study, whether using a textbook or the FOA Online Reference Guide. Premises cabling consists of copper and fiber cabling and wireless, mainly considering cabling for wireless for the premises cabling technician. We have broken the KSAs into 4 categories: cabling systems overview, copper, fiber and wireless.

Knowledge	Cabling Systems	Copper Cabling	Fiber Optic Cabling	Wireless
Overview	What are cabling systems Where are they used	Types of copper cabling systems Where they are used Legacy systems	Where is fiber used and why What applications does it support	Why use wireless How does it fit into a structured cabling system
Jargon	Cabling systems jargon and standards	Copper cabling systems jargon and standards	Fiber optic cabling systems jargon and standards	Wireless systems jargon and standards
Communications Systems	What types of communications systems use structured cabling	How do communications systems use copper cabling Power over Ethernet	How do communications systems use fiber optic cabling	How do communications systems use wireless

Knowledge	Cabling Systems	Copper Cabling	Fiber Optic Cabling	Wireless
Cabling	Generic use of cabling	Types of copper cabling used in premises cabling systems	Types of fiber optic cabling used in premises cabling systems	Types of cabling used by wireless in premises cabling systems
Termination & Splicing	NA	Where connectors and punch-downs are used Relevant performance specifications Hardware needed (e.g. patch panels, patchcords, etc.)	Where connectors and splices are used Types of connectors and splices and applications Relevant performance specifications Hardware needed (e.g. patch panels, patchcords, etc.)	Relevant cabling to connect wireless access points
Testing		Test requirements for UTP cable certification or verification Troubleshooting	Microscope inspection Visual tracing and fault location Insertion loss testing OTDR testing Troubleshooting	

Knowledge	Cabling Systems	Copper Cabling	Fiber Optic Cabling	Wireless
Design	Evaluating communications system requirements Designing the proper cable plant Layout Choosing components Loss budgets Documentation	As specific for copper cabling	As specific for fiber optic cabling	As specific for cabling for wireless and location of wireless access points
Installation	Evaluating needs based on cable plant design Planning for the installation Safety Eye Safety Tool safety Chemical safety Disposal of materials Basic knowledge of Codes, standards, and Regulations Performing the installation (including grounding and bonding, firestopping, etc.)	As specific for copper cabling	As specific for fiber optic cabling	As specific for cabling for wireless and wireless access points

| | Cabling Systems | | |
	Copper Cabling	Fiber Optic Cabling	Wireless
Knowledge			
Skills	Copper Cable Pulling cable Placing cable in trays, J-hooks, etc. Preparing cable for splicing or termination Punchdowns Preparing cable for punchdowns Color codes Maintaining performance at punchdowns Termination Preparing cables for termination Installing connectors Maintaining performance at connectors Testing Certification testing Verification Testing TDR testing	Fiber Optic Cable Attaching pulling eye and rope to a cable Pulling cable Preparing cable for splicing or termination Splicing Preparing cable for splicing Mechanical splicing Fusion splicing Termination Identifying connectors Preparing cables for termination Installing connectors Inspecting connectors Testing Microscope inspection Visual tracing and fault location Insertion loss testing OTDR testing	Wireless AP Cabling (Fiber or copper as appropriate)

Knowledge	Cabling Systems	Copper Cabling	Fiber Optic Cabling	Wireless
Abilities	Good eyesight with color rendition Good hand-eye coordination Be able to use hand and power tools Analytical skills Follow directions Patience Work in adverse conditions			

Appendix B
Optical LANs (OLANs)

Introduction

Optical LANs (local area networks) have been around since the mid-1980s, but in the last few years they have benefited from the worldwide move to install fiber to the home. With over 100 million FTTH subscribers, FTTH has become a market driven by the economies of scale and costs have plummeted. It did not take long for designers to understand that FTTH, especially as used in multi-dwelling units, was similar to typical LANs. Much as LANs based on telco PBX architectures became the first standard for LANs in the 1980s, telco FTTH architectures, especially PONs (passive optical networks), are being adopted for the next generation of LANs. Here you will find some history and an explanation of how this new generation of telco architecture is being widely adopted.

The Development of LANs and Premises Cabling

Networks that allowed computers to communicate with other computers and peripherals have been around for a long time. They evolved in two directions - wide area networks using phone lines and then the Internet, and local area networks (LANs) where most connected devices were in a building or campus. Networking PCs began seriously in the mid 1980s with many competing networks, most proprietary: Ethernet, IBM Token Ring, DECnet, WangNet, etc. mostly using higher bandwidth coax cable or shielded twisted pair. Over time, Ethernet, developed by Xerox Palo Alto Research Labs, became the most popular. AT&T recognized the need for computer networks and created StarLAN using telephone wire. Not long afterwards, two people left Xerox PARC and started Synoptics, originally to do LANs over fiber, but they discovered balanced transmission on unshielded twisted pair copper cables and created LattisNet which was close to what became 10BASE-T.

Local area networks (LANs) used to connect computers in a premises (indoor building) environment have been mostly based on standardized structured cabling. Structured cabling standards were developed around 1990 based on a 1982 AT&T survey of a small number of users of phone private switches (PBXs or private branch exchanges) that showed that most users were less than 300 feet (about 100m) from the switch. Using this information, a structured cabling architecture based on backbone cabling to local telecom rooms containing LAN hubs or switches that served users over copper cables was adopted. Early additions to the standard allowed for longer backbone distances using optical fiber.

Here is a diagram of early structured cabling, appropriately using a graphic from the era. Note the use of telecom nomenclature.

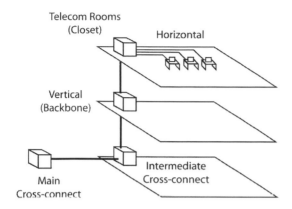

Structured cabling LAN

Over time, Ethernet network speeds grew from 10 to 100MB/s and then 1Gb/s. Fiber was quickly recognized as a simpler way to upgrade to higher speeds and provide longer backbone connections. Both multimode and singlemode fiber were added to the cabling standards for backbones with longer lengths and multimode was added to the horizontal link but still with the same 100m length limit.

The additional link length capability of fiber was later recognized by allowing a "centralized fiber" architecture in the standards. Here fiber connects the desktop directly without the electronics in the telecom closet (renamed telecom room in later versions of the standard.) Since fiber needs no intermediate electronics, the cost of equipment drops and the need for power, AC and grounds - or even the space allocated for the equipment (the telecom room) - means the cost of equipping telecom rooms goes away, easily offsetting the higher cost of the fiber electronics needed to interface to the connected device. The cost of the fiber cabling, meanwhile, had dropped and copper increased, so the cabling cost itself was often less for fiber than copper.

Meanwhile, wireless (WiFi) had become more capable of handling typical network traffic and users had begun migrating from desktop computers to laptops, tablets and smartphones using wireless, so architectures to support WiFi were being used in addition to desktop cabling.

Here is the current day architecture of centralized fiber compared to normal structured cabling and the addition of WiFi access points.

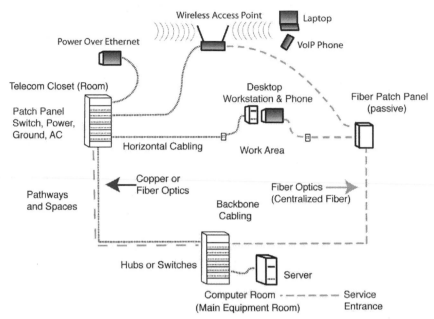

Current structured cabling diagram

The Bandwidth Issue

To keep up with the needs to transfer more and more data, Ethernet advanced to higher speeds. 1 - 10 -100Mb/s came quickly and with little pain, although users had to upgrade numerous times from Cat 3 - 4 - 5 -5e - 6A) at very high expense. But 1Gb/s and 10Gb/s stressed the unshielded twisted pair cable preferred by most users. Transceivers had to become more sophisticated, power hungry and cabling needed more bandwidth.

Cat 5, practically the only cable needed in the 1990s, was almost OK for 1Gb/s Ethernet using new types of transceivers, but a small upgrade to "enhanced" Cat 5 or Cat 5e made it good for another few years. Cat 6, yet higher bandwidth UTP, never had a network that called for it and it was inadequate for 10Gb/s Ethernet, which led to the development of Cat 6A (augmented Cat 6).

The speed upgrade to Ethernet at 10Gb/s created a new set of problems. UTP copper cabling, the basic cabling of structured cabling, required continual upgrades to meet the needs of faster networks. As speeds exceeded 1Gb/s, copper development was much slower than fiber and links required much higher power to support the higher bandwidth signals. Proposals to develop a new cable -Cat 8 - for higher speed networks like 40G Ethernet over short distances are being evaluated.

Multimode fiber also required upgrading for faster networks. While multimode fiber had been engineered for higher and higher bandwidth capability (OM3 and OM4 varieties) to maintain at least 100m link lengths, the power budget of these systems using 850 nm VCSELs had dropped to only about 2 dB, hardly enough to accommodate the connectors on either end, while most links had two or more patch panel connections. Then, when 40Gb/s and 100Gb/s Ethernet was developed, it required multiple parallel links at 10Gb/s to work on multimode fiber. 40Gb Ethernet required 8 fibers (4 in each direction) while 100G Ethernet required 20 fibers (10 in each direction) usually using 24 because MTP/MPO connectors are designed around 12 fibers or 24 fibers per connector.

Many users found using parallel fiber connections with limited distance capability much less appealing than using wavelength-division multiplexing (WDM) over a pair of singlemode fibers to get 100Gb/s. Those singlemode fibers were easily capable of supporting terabits/s data. If one looks at the capability of various types of media, this graph sums it up:

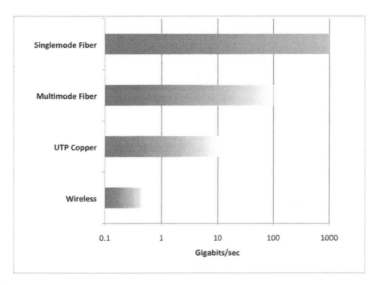

Speeds For Various LAN Media

At the same time, new fiber to the home (FTTH) architectures using a passive optical network (PON) or point-to-point (P2P) links became cost-effective for broadband connections. In the first 5 years of active FTTH installations, almost 100 million homes, apartments and businesses were directly connected on fiber. Such high volume means prices dropped enough to make the cost of a singlemode fiber link as cheap as copper, or even cheaper when singlemode fiber's higher bandwidth capacity allowed for multiple users to share one fiber link.

Once suppliers and users realized that a premises LAN was not much different than an apartment building (called a MDU - multi-dwelling unit - in FTTH jargon) the FTTH architecture began being used in large LANs. By "large" we mean they started with LANs covering large geographic areas like a campus or large building as well as "large" in numbers of users, typically hundreds or thousands of users.

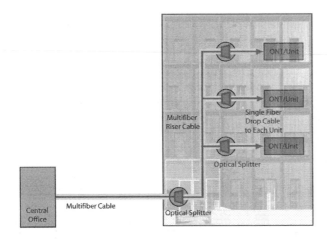

FTTH in a Multi-Dwelling Unit

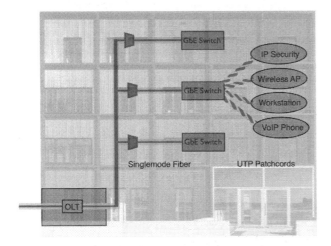

Passive Optical OLAN in Office Building

These applications became known as "passive optical LANs" (POLs) when using FTTH PON technology and "fiber to the office" (FTTO) when using P2P links. Collectively they are being called OLANs for "optical LANs). OLANs are based on international standards for FTTH but are being considered to be included in the structured cabling standards in the future.

Both FTTO and POL use multiport mini-switches at the user outlet. POLs are designed for triple play services (voice, data and video) but usually only carry the services needed by the user, typically Ethernet. FTTO outlets are usually multiport Ethernet. Data ports are generally Gigabit Ethernet but upgrades to higher bit rates may be done. User terminals may have POE (power over Ethernet) available using the local powering for the ONT or switch. OLANs are ideal solutions for many networks. They are essentially not distance limited, so they are ideal for large buildings (convention centers, airports, libraries, sports facilities, hospitals, etc.) or campuses. They scale easily to large networks, with networks of 16,000 users already installed. They use little space compared to traditional structured cabling networks. Not only are telecom rooms not needed, but the entrance facility electronics are small too. And the networks easily accommodate very high data usage; some can handle 10-20Gb/s connections to the outside world. POLs also have another advantage in security. Since they broadcast through a PON splitter to all users, each signal must be encrypted, adding a layer of security for the network.

Here are some examples of Optical LANs.

Fiber To The Office (FTTO)

Fiber to the office is a simple development of centralized fiber in structured cabling architecture, except it uses lower cost components designed for FTTH. The network for Terminal 3 at the Dubai Airport was designed by Cliff Walker for FTTO. It uses P2P links to 4 port switches. FTTO was chosen in part because of the sheer size of the terminal that made copper or multimode fiber unfeasible. This architecture is similar to centralized fiber optics in structured cabling standards except it uses FTTH hardware, including singlemode fiber. Here is Cliff Walker's paper on this FTTO application.

Passive Optical LANs (POLs)

The new San Diego central library encompasses 9 floors of library and technical high school. There are over 1000 drops with 4 port ONTs that support 4000 users. Sandia National Labs in Los Alamos, NM is much bigger. The passive optical LAN there covers 13,000+ users (50k ports) in 265 buildings. It cost $15M, with savings of $20M expected over a traditional structured cabling system. Using a POL reduced energy costs by 65% and created $80,000 in recycled copper cabling.

How Does An OLAN Differ From Traditional LANs?

Traditional LANs on structured cabling have limited distance links and are broken into backbone and horizontal sections. If implemented in copper or a combination of fiber and copper, they will have intermediate electronics in a telecom room. OLANs centralize all the network electronics, eliminating the telecom closet, and only use intermediate patching points where one connects larger fiber count cables to drop cables. OLANs implemented in singlemode fiber are not distance limited for the typical LANs. In fact one could build a metropolitan LAN using OLAN equipment considering the distance capability of FTTH systems.

Advantages/Disadvantages of OLANs

Advantages

- Both FTTO and POLs use SM fiber with no bandwidth limitations from the cable plant
- They take advantage of the technology and economics of FTTH with millions of installations
- Each work area switch needs only one singlemode fiber (POL) or two singlemode fibers (FTTO)
- The smaller number of cables and smaller cables makes for simpler, cheaper installation
- Both avoid masses of UTP copper cabling and required hardware (cable trays, patch panels, telecom rooms)
- POL switches are designed to connect directly with incoming telecom/ Internet services as well as Ethernet devices at 10Gb/s or more
- Mini-switches and ONTs connect to all user devices (PCs, APs) over standard UTP "Cat 5" patchcords – no media converters required
- Voice, data and video are easily accommodated as is anything that runs over Ethernet
- OLANs have more distance capability, 10km or more, allowing one LAN to cover campus or metropolitan areas
- They are about as "Future Proof" as you can get
- Cost is lower than traditional LAN architecture using structured cabling, both initial expense and operating costs, especially since POLs use ~1/5 as much power as traditional LANs

Disadvantages

- Generally best for larger numbers of users (100-200+) although new

equipment may make smaller LANs cost effective
- Requires installing singlemode fiber (but using prefab cables or prepolished/splice connectors simplify termination)
- Requires SM test equipment (OLTS is not a problem but requires a very high resolution SM OTDR which would not be needed for most installations)

Perhaps the best comparison is the installation of traditional UTP cabling versus the installation of singlemode fibers to a work area.

Here is a comparison of three types of fiber optic cables for a 4-port OLAN switch compared to the UTP Cat 5E cables to support horizontal runs for 4 users.

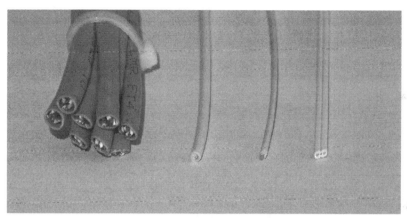

Fiber & copper cables required to connect to work area. On the left, 8 Cat 5E cables. Next a 3mm simplex singlemode fiber cable, a 2mm cable and a special ruggedized FTTH drop cable with 2 fibers.

Optical fiber has so much less bulk, one does not need giant cable trays like in the hotel to the left. Even the conduit used in the San Diego Central Library for UTP cables dwarfs the simplex fiber optic cable needed to each work area.
Where Do OLANs Make Sense?

OLANs work best in larger LANs where the savings will be greatest. Generally, any LAN with a few hundred users will benefit from an OLAN. Based on data from CI&M magazine, that means that ~45% of all LANs which include ~98% of all users are likely to benefit from OLANs. New equipment may make LANs of 100 users or less feasible with OLANs.

Typical users would be:

- Corporations

- Public buildings, airports, convention centers
- Hotels and convention centers, casinos
- Hospitals
- Schools, campuses
- Municipal networks
- Government and military facilities (some have standardized on OLANs already)

Understanding Passive Optical LANs

Passive optical LANs use standard FTTH architecture and protocols which are quite different from typical LANs. In a Ethernet LAN with structured cabling architecture, Ethernet switches in the main equipment room connect to routers for Internet connections and servers in the corporate data center to provide data for users. Users are connected on a multi-link system that uses backbone cabling to connect the main switches to local switches in the telecom rooms near the users. Users will then be connected over horizontal cabling, usually UTP which runs from the telecom room to the work area. The telecom room requires uninterruptible, data-quality power, special data grounding and usually air conditioning to keep the temperature in the telecom room under control.

Passive optical LANs use internationally standardized systems called GPON (Gigabit PON) or EPON (Ethernet PON) with GPON the most popular now (October 2013).

Type	Description	International Standard
GPON	Gigabit PON	TU-T G.984
EPON	Ethernet PON	IEEE 802.3ah (1 Gb/s) IEEE 802.3av (10Gb/s)

A GPON system is shown below.

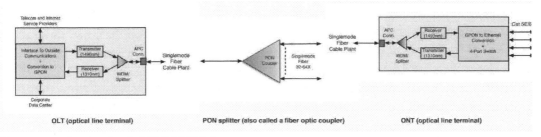

OLT (optical line terminal)   PON splitter (also called a fiber optic coupler)   ONT (optical line terminal)

Diagram of a typical GPON POL

A POL needs nothing but passive components - fiber optic cabling and a splitter - between the main equipment room OLT and the work area ONT. Signals are transmitted simultaneously in both directions at two different wavelengths using wavelength-division multiplexing (WDM) so each work area needs only a single singlemode fiber to connect to the network.

FTTH passive optical networks use fiber optic splitters to split out a downstream signal to a number of users, usually 32, reducing the complexity of the electronics and the bulk of the cabling, plus it spits the cost of the downstream electronics by the number of users, making the cost per user much lower, even lower than a link using copper cables between Ethernet ports. Upstream, the POL uses the coupler as a combiner - combining the incoming signals into a single fiber to connect to the OLT. Each user work area has a ONT that uses an inexpensive 1310nm laser for upstream signals. In both directions the system will work with ~13 to 28dB loss and most of the loss will be in the coupler. With a design specification of 10km links, POLs offer maximum flexibility to users spread over a large geographic area, not just a campus but large manufacturing plants or even a small city.

The PON splitter serves basically the same purpose as a switch but requires no power, ground or air conditioning and takes a fraction of the space. The splitter can be mounted on a wall, above a ceiling or under a desk. Splitters can be cascaded for the 32X split ratio to split nearer work areas to reduce cabling.

PON Splitters

Splitters are passive optical branching devices which couple fibers in multiples, leading to their other name - couplers. They can be made from planar waveguides (flat pieces of optical material that geometrically divide the light as it passes through the material) or from fused fiber bundles (fused biconically tapered fiber couplers are made by wrapping fibers together and heating to melting temperatures in a controlled manner.)

Splitters are bidirectional. In the illustration above, light coming in one direction will be split into four roughly equal outputs, while light coming from the other direction will be combined into the one fiber on the other side of the splitter - effectively becoming a combiner.

Splitters are available in 1:2, 1:4, 1:8, 1:16, 1:32 configurations. PON architectures are generally based on a maximum of 1:32 split. High split ratios are usually made by planar waveguide devices, while fused biconical tapered fiber couplers have smaller split ratios.

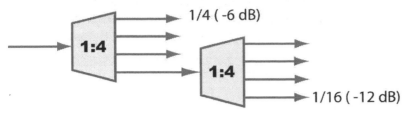

POL splitters can be cascaded to reduce fiber needs by putting splitters nearer the users' work areas.

Splitters can be cascaded to achieve the desired split ratio, e.g. a 1:4 splitter then four 1:4 splitters is 1:16. Needless to say, if you split the light from one fiber into several fibers, the amount of light is divided, so the light in the several fibers is lower by the split ratio. In fact the loss is 3 dB per 2x split (3 dB is a 50% loss) plus a certain amount of "excess loss" caused by the inefficiency of the splitter - loss inside the splitter caused by the mechanism of the splitting.

Split Ratio	1:2	1:4	1:8	1:16	1:32
Ideal Loss (dB)	3	6	9	12	15
Actual Loss (dB)	4	7	11	15	19
Excess Loss (dB)	1	1	2	3	4

If we split the downstream signal to 32 users, how does each user get their specific data? The data is transmitted downstream (at 2.4Gb/s in GPON, currently the most popular FTTH network used for POLs) using time division multiplexing and - this is important - each user's data is encrypted to prevent other users from intercepting their data. The combination of fiber cabling and encryption makes POLs highly desirable for those concerned about secrecy and wiretapping. The downstream multiplexing can dynamically allocate bandwidth as needed. Upstream signals in GPON are at 1.2Gb/s. Higher bit rate GPON and EPON (PONs that use Ethernet protocols) are being developed.

ONTs in LANs usually incorporate 4 gigabit Ethernet ports (1000base-T over Cat 5e patchcords) but other options are available. A triple-play ONT from FTTH gives voice/data/video outputs. Multiple POTs phone ports, more or less Ethernet ports, etc. are available from various vendors. The ONT is powered locally and can incorporate power over Ethernet (PoE) to power local devices like WiFi access points, voice over IP (VoIP) phones or video cameras. Having local PoE provides the convenience of PoE without the high power losses encountered in long horizontal cable runs.

Those experienced in typical Ethernet LAN hardware may have trouble believing the hardware for POLs. The OLT that connects all the users also includes connections for outside services (telco and Internet). In fact, most OLTs are designed for one or more 10Gb/s connections, hardly the typical slow T1-T3 or 10-50Mb/s available through routers for most LANs. the size of the hardware is also amazing as shown below.

A small rack mounted system can support 2000+ connections with splitters which connects 8000+ users via 4-port switches. Compare that to the room full of Ethernet switches to support 8000 users! Even smaller units are available to support fewer users. At the work area, small switches about the size of a cable modem or DSL modem are common, but switches that fit in a wall outlet are also available.

Security And Reliability
POLs are adapted from telco systems that are designed for 99.999% reliability, at least 10X normal LAN components. UPS power is required only at the main equipment room and at the user work area if desired. No power is needed at any intermediate point like traditional structured cabling requires for switches in a telecom room. Redundancy can be built into systems using splitters with two inputs instead of one, with each input connected to a separate OLT for backup.

As mentioned above, signals are encrypted downstream and systems that encrypt upstream and monitor fibers to detect tapping are available for high security areas.

Designing and Installing OLANs

Most buildings designed in the last 20 years have been designed around structured cabling with large areas set aside for pathways and spaces, most of which are not necessary for OLANs. Some OLAN users have actually recovered spaces allocated for telecom rooms. Cable trays emptied when obsolete UTP cables are removed for recycling can be left since removing them is costly. Older buildings that were designed before structured cabling standards that have always been difficult to install cabling systems are much easier, obviously.

As we mentioned above, OLANs are using only singlemode cables that are easy to install but require special termination procedures (generally prepolished/splice connections) or using prefab cable assemblies. Many of the components are similar to those developed to ease installation of FTTH (as shown here). Manufacturers have also developed special hardware to simplify the prefab cable plant installation.

Testing POLs is easy for insertion loss but requires special knowledge with OTDRs as they splitter can be confusing. Cable plants with splitters have different OTDR traces upstream and downstream so techs should be trained on the special needs of POL testing with OTDRs.

Additional information on POLs and FTTH PONs is online in the FOA Guide.

Training And Certification

FOA has two OLAN certifications, an Optical LAN (OLAN) specialist certification (CFOS/L) for CFOTs with training available from FOA approved schools and an Application Specialist (CFAS/L) available online. An OLAN self-study program is also available on Fiber U, FOA's free online training site.

Appendix C
Specifications For Fiber Optic Networks

Per current standards and specs, maximum supportable distances and attenuation for optical fiber applications by fiber type.

Multimode Fiber Network Specifications (- means Not Applicable)

Application	Parameter	Multimode Fiber Type							
		62.5/125 µm TIA 492AAAA (OM1)		50/125 µm TIA 492AAAB (OM2)		850 nm laser-optimized 50/125 µm TIA 492AAAC (OM3)		850 nm laser-optimized 50/125 µm TIA 492AAAD (OM4)	
	Nominal wavelength (nm)	850	1300	850	1300	850	1300	850	1300
	Channel attenuation (dB)	4.0	-	4.0	-	4.0	-	4.0	-
Ethernet 10/100BASE-SX	Supportable distance m (ft)	300 (984)	-	300 (984)	-	300 (984)	-	300 (984)	-

Ethernet type	Metric	Multimode Fiber Type							
		(1)	(2)	(3)	(4)	(5)	(6)	(7)	(8)
Ethernet 100BASE-FX	Channel attenuation (dB)	-	11.0	-	6.0	-	6.0	-	6.0
	Supportable distance m (ft)	-	2000 (6560)	-	2000 (6560)	-	2000 (6560)	-	2000 (6560)
Ethernet 1000BASE-SX	Channel attenuation (dB)	2.6	-	3.6	-	4.5	-	4.8	-
	Supportable distance m (ft)	275 (900)	-	550 (1804)	-	800 (2625)	-	880 (2887)	-
Ethernet 1000BASE-LX	Channel attenuation (dB)	-	2.3	-	2.3	-	2.3	-	2.3
	Supportable distance m (ft)	-	550 (1804)	-	550 (1804)	-	550 (1804)	-	550 (1804)
Ethernet 10GBASE-S	Channel attenuation (dB)	2.4	-	2.3	-	2.6	-	3.1	-
	Supportable distance m (ft)	33 (108)	-	82 (269)	-	300 (984)	-	450 (1476)	-
Ethernet 10GBASE-LX4	Channel attenuation (dB)	-	2.5	-	2.0	-	2.0	-	2.0
	Supportable distance m (ft)	-	300 (984)	-	300 (984)	-	300 (984)	-	300 (984)

Application	Parameter	Multimode Fiber Type							
		OM1		OM2		OM3		OM4	
		850	1300	850	1300	850	1300	850	1300
	Nominal wavelength (nm)	850	1300	850	1300	850	1300	850	1300
Ethernet 40GBASE-SR4	Channel attenuation (dB)					1.9		1.9	
	Supportable distance m (ft)					100 (328)		125 (410)	
Ethernet 100GBASE-SR10	Channel attenuation (dB)					1.9		1.9	
	Supportable distance m (ft)					100 (328)		125 (410)	
1G Fibre Channel 100-MX-SN-I (1062 Mbaud)	Channel attenuation (dB)	3.0	-	3.9	-	4.6	-	4.6	-
	Supportable distance m (ft)	300 (984)	-	500 (1640)	-	860 (2822)	-	860 (2822)	-

		Multimode Fiber Type						
2G Fibre Channel 200-MX-SN-I (2125 Mbaud)	Channel attenuation (dB)	2.1	–	2.6	–	3.3	3.3	–
	Supportable distance m (ft)	150 (492)	–	300 (984)	–	500 (1640)	500 (1640)	–
4G Fibre Channel 400-MX-SN-I (4250 Mbaud)	Channel attenuation (dB)	1.8	–	2.1	–	2.9	3.0	–
	Supportable distance m (ft)	70 (230)	–	150 (492)	–	380 (1247)	400 (1312)	–
10G Fibre Channel 1200-MX-SN-I (10512 Mbaud)	Channel attenuation (dB)	2.4	–	2.2	–	2.6	2.6	–
	Supportable distance m (ft)	33 (108)	–	82 (269)	–	300 (984)	300 (984)	–
16G Fibre Channel 1600-MX-SN (10512 Mbaud)	Channel attenuation (dB)	–	–	1.6	–	1.9	1..9	–
	Supportable distance m (ft)	–	–	35 (115)	–	100 (328)	125 (410)	–
FDDI PMD ANSI X3.166	Channel attenuation (dB)	–	11.0	–	6.0	–	6.0	6.0
	Supportable distance m (ft)	–	2000 (6560)	–	2000 (6560)	–	2000 (6560)	2000 (6560)

Singlemode Fiber Network Specifications (- means Not Applicable)

Application	Parameter	Single-mode TIA 492CAAA (OS1) or TIA 492CAAB (OS2)	
		1310	1550
	Nominal wavelength (nm)	1310	1550
Ethernet 1000BASE-LX	Channel attenuation (dB)	4.5	-
	Supportable distance m (ft)	5000 (16405)	-
Ethernet 10GBASE-LX4	Channel attenuation (dB)	6.3	-
	Supportable distance m (ft)	10000 (32810)	-
Ethernet 10GBASE-L	Channel attenuation (dB)	6.2	-
	Supportable distance m (ft)	10000 (32810)	-
Ethernet 10GBASE-E	Channel attenuation (dB)	-	11.0
	Supportable distance m (ft)	-	40000 (131240)

Application	Parameter	Single-mode	
Ethernet 40GBASE-LR4	Channel attenuation (dB)	6.7	
	Supportable distance m (ft)	10000 (32810)	
Ethernet 100GBASE-LR4	Channel attenuation (dB)	6.3	
	Supportable distance m (ft)	10000 (32810)	
1G Fibre Channel 100-SM-LC-L	Channel attenuation (dB)	7.8	-
	Supportable distance m (ft)	10000 (32810)	-
2G Fibre Channel 200-SM-LC-L	Channel attenuation (dB)	7.8	-
	Supportable distance m (ft)	10000 (32810)	-
4G Fibre Channel 400-SM-LC-M	Channel attenuation (dB)	4.8	-
	Supportable distance m (ft)	4000 (13124)	-
4G Fibre Channel 400-SM-LC-L	Channel attenuation (dB)	7.8	-
	Supportable distance m (ft)	10000 (32810)	-

Application	Parameter	Single-mode OS1 or OS2	
8G Fibre Channel 800-SM-LC-L (4250 Mbaud)	Channel attenuation (dB)	6.4	-
	Supportable distance m (ft)	10000 (32810)	-
10G Fibre Channel 1200-SM-LL-L	Channel attenuation (dB)	6.0	-
	Supportable distance m (ft)	10000 (32810)	-
16G Fibre Channel 1600-SM-LC-L	Channel attenuation (dB)	6.4	-
	Supportable distance m (ft)	10000 (32810)	-
FDDI SMF-PMD ANSI X3.184	Channel attenuation (dB)	10.0	-
	Supportable distance m (ft)	10000 (32810)	-

(- means Not Applicable)

Specifications For Legacy Fiber Optic Networks

A listing of many fiber optic LANs and links available in the last 30 years, with basic operational specs.

Application	Wavelength	Max distance (m) for fiber type			Link Margin (dB) for fiber type		
		62.5/125	50/125	SM	62.5	50	SM
10Base-F	850	2000	2000	NS	12.5	7.8	NS
FOIRL	850	2000	NS	NS	8	NS	NS
Token Ring 4/16	850	2000	2000	NS	13	8.3	NS
Demand Priority (100VG-AnyLAN)	850	500	500	NS	7.5	2.8	NS
Demand Priority (100VG-AnyLAN)	1300	2000	2000	NS	7.0	2.3	NS
100Base-FX (Fast Ethernet)	1300	2000	2000	NS	11	6.3	NS
10/100Base-SX	850	300	300	NS	4.0	4.0	NS
FDDI	1300	2000	2000	40,000	11.0	6.3	10-32
FDDI (low cost)	1300	500	500	NA	7.0	2.3	NA
ATM 52	1300	3000	3000	15,000	10	5.3	7-12
ATM 155	1300	2000	2000	15,000	10	5.3	7-12
ATM 155	850(laser)	1000	1000	NA	7.2	7.2	NA
ATM 622	1300	500	500	15,000	6.0	1.3	7-12
ATM 622	850(laser)	300	300	NA	4.0	4.0	NA

Application	Wavelength	Max distance (m) for fiber type			Link Margin (dB) for fiber type		
		62.5/125	50/125	SM	62.5	50	SM
Fibre Channel 1062	850(laser)	300	500	NA	4.0	4.0	NA
Fibre Channel 1062	1300	NA	NA	10,000	NA	NA	6-14
1000Base-SX	850(laser)	220	550	NA	3.2	3.9	NA
1000Base-LX	1300	550	550	5000	4.0	3.5	4.7
ESCON	1300	3000	NS	20,000	11	NS	16

NA = Not Applicable

NS = Not Specified. Most LANs and links not specified to run on SM fiber have media converters available to allow them to run on SM fiber.

Appendix D
Definitions of Terms

A

Absorption: That portion of fiber optic attenuation resulting of conversion of optical power to heat.

ACR: attenuation to crosstalk ratio, a measure of how much more signal than noise exists in the link, by comparing the attenuated signal from one pair at the receiver to the crosstalk induced in the same pair.

Adapters: a type of balun that physically allows one connector to mate to another.

ADO: Auxiliary Disconnect Outlet

Alien Crosstalk: Crosstalk from a pair in one cable to the same pair in another adjacent cable.

Analog: An electrical signal that carries information in a continuously varying format.

ATM: Asynchronous Transfer Mode

Attenuation: the reduction of signal strength over distance.

Attenuator: A device that reduces signal power by inducing loss.

AUI: Attachment Unit Interface, Ethernet tap on coax.

Average power: The average over time of a modulated signal.

B

Backbone: cable that connects communications closets, entrance facilities and buildings. (Cabling Subsystem 1 in new TIA 568 nomenclature).

Balanced transmission: sending signals of opposite polarity on each wire in a pair to maximize bandwidth and minimize interference. Used with all UTP cable.

Balun: a device that adapts one cabling type to another, including physical layout, impedance and connecting balanced to unbalanced cables.

Bandwidth: the frequency spectrum required or provided by communications networks.

Baud rate: Rate of signal transmission (bps) Bits per Second.

Baud: for phone modems, it refers to the data rate, but in networks, it is the actual modulation rate which may not be the same as the data rate if encoding schemes are used.

BD: Building Distributor

BDN: Building Distribution Network

Bend radius: minimum radius a cable can be bent without permanent damage.

BER: Bit Error Rate

BIT: Binary Digit, An electrical or optical pulse that carries information, a single piece of digital information, a "1" or "0".

Bit-error rate (BER): The fraction of data bits transmitted that are received in error.

BIX: Northern Telecom proprietary premises cross-connect system.

Block, punchdown block: devices used for interconnection of cables.

Bluetooth: Limited distance wireless network, IEEE 802.15.

BNC: Bayonet CXC coax connectors.

Bonding: a permanent electrical connection.

Bridge: a device that connects two or more sets of telephone wires.

Bus: a network where all computers are connected by a single (usually coax) cable. Bus architecture can also be implemented with a hub and star configuration.

Byte: Eight or sixteen Bit Binary word.

C

Cable tray: a channel system used to hold and support communications cables.

Cable: One or more conductors or fibers enclosed in protective coverings and strength members.

Capacitance: the ability of a conductor to store charge.

Category-Rated unshielded twisted pair (UTP) cables: Four twisted pair UTP cable rated for frequency performance.

Category 3: the UTP cable specified for signals up to 16 MHz, commonly used for telephones. (ISO/IEC Class C).

Category 4: the UTP cable specified for signals up to 20 MHz, obsolete.

Category 5/5E: the UTP cable specified for signals up to 100 MHz, commonly used for all LANs. (ISO/IEC Class D).

Category 6/6A: the UTP cable specified for signals up to 500 MHz, commonly used for > gigabit LANs. (ISO/IEC Class E).

Category 7: Erroneous nomenclature for ISO/IEC Class F STP cable, not part of TIA standards.

CATV: community antenna television, usually delivered by coax cable or HFC(hybrid fiber-coax) networks.

CBC: Communications Building Cable

CCITT: Consultants Committee for International Telephone and Telegraph.

CCTV: closed circuit television, commonly used for security.

CD: Campus Distributor

CDDI: Copper Distribution Data Interface

CEMA: Canadian Electrical Manufacturers Association

Certification Tester: Tests wiremap, length, attenuation and crosstalk per standards.

Client: the computer that operates in a network using programs and data stored in a server.

CM: Communications Cables

CMG: Communications Cable General Rated

CMP: Communications Cable Plenum Rated

CMR: Communications Cable Riser Rated

CMX: Communications Cable Residential Rated

COAX, CXC : Coaxial Cable

Coax: a type of cable that uses a central conductor, insulation, outer conductor/shield and jacket, used for high frequency communications like CCTV or CATV.

Conduit: special pipe used to carry cables. May be metal or plastic, solid or flexible.

Connector: the attachment on the end of a cable that allows interconnection to other cables.

Connection Point A: New TIA 568 designation for main cross connect or equipment room.

Connection Point C: New TIA 568 designation for telecom room.

Connection Point D: New TIA 568 designation for work area outlet.

CP: Consolidation Point

CPE: Customer Premises Equipment

CPI: Component Premises Interface

Crimper: a tool used to install insulation-displacement plugs (IDC) on UTP cable or crimp-style connectors on coax cable.

Crossed pair: a pair of wires in a UTP cable that have two pairs cross-connected in error.

CSA: Canadian Standards Association

CSMA/CD: carrier sensing multiple access / collision detection, the protocol of Ethernet and other networks using bus or star architecture, that controls access to the LAN.

Current loop: transmission using variable current to carry information, like a simple analog telephone.

D

Decibel (dB): A unit of measurement of optical power which indicates relative power on a logarithmic scale, sometimes called dBr. dB=10 log (power ratio)

dBm: Electrical: decibels in reference to Milliwatts , 0dBm = 1 mw base measurement.

dBm: Optical: optical power referenced to 1 milliwatt.

DC: Direct Current

DD: Distribution Device

Delay skew: the maximum difference of propagation time in all pairs of a cable.

Dial tone: the tone heard in a phone when the receiver is picked up, indicating the line is available for dialing.

Dielectric: an insulator, used to protect copper wires in cable.

Digital: signals where the information is in the form of digital bits - 1's and 0's.

Dispersion: The temporal spreading of a pulse in an optical waveguide. May be caused by modal or chromatic effects.

DIW: "D" Inside Wire

DMARC: Demarcation Point

DTE: Data Terminal Equipment

DTMF: dual tone multifrequency, or tone dialing used on modern phones, where discrete tones indicate numbers.

DVO: Data Voice Outlet

E

EIA/TIA 568 standard: a voluntary interoperability standard developed by vendors to insure interoperability of equipment used on network cabling. The international equivalent is ISO/IEC 11801.

EIA/TIA: Electronics Industry Association/Telecommunications Industry Association, a vendor-based group that writes voluntary interoperability standards for communications and electronics.

EL-FEXT: Equal Level Far End Crosstalk, crosstalk ar the far end with signals of equal level being transmitted.

EMI: Electromagnetic Interference

ESCON: IBM storage center network.

ESD: Electrostatic Discharge

Ethernet: A network standard widely used for computer networks. Many standards exist for Ethernet over various speeds and types of media. Examples:

    10 BASE 2: 10 MB/S Ethernet on Thinnet Cable

    10 BASE 5: 10 MB/S Ethernet on Thicknet Cable

    10 BASE F: 1O MB/S Ethernet on Fiber Optic cable

    10 BASE T: 10 MB/S Ethernet Cat. 3 or better Twisted Pair Cable

    100 BASE T: 100 MB/S Fast Ethernet on Cat. 5

    1000 BASE LX: Gigabit Ethernet on optical fiber at 1300 nm

    1000 BASE SX: Gigabit Ethernet on optical fiber at 850 nm

    1000 BASE T: Gigabit Ethernet on Cat 5e UTP

    10GBASE-T: 10 Gigabit Ethernet on Cat 6A UTP

    10GBASE-CX4: 10 Gigabit Ethernet on coax

    10GBASE-S: 10 Gigabit Ethernet on MM at 850 nm w/VCSELs

    10GBASE-LX4: 10 Gigabit Ethernet on MM or SM using WDM

    10GBASE-L: 10 Gigabit Ethernet on SM at 1310 nm for 10 km

    10GBASE-LRM: 10 Gigabit Ethernet on MM at 1310 nm w/FP lasers

    10GBASE-E: 10 Gigabit Ethernet on SM at 1550 nm for 40 km

    40GBASE-SR4: 40 Gigabit Ethernet on MM at 850 nm w/VCSELs

    40GBASE-LR4: 40 Gigabit Ethernet on MM at 1310 nm w/FP lasers

    100GBASE-SR10: 100 Gigabit Ethernet on MM at 850 nm w/VCSELs

    100GBASE-LR4: 100 Gigabit Ethernet on MM at 1310 nm w/FP lasers

F

F Series Conn.: Threaded RG59 CXC Connector
FDM: Frequency Division Multiplexing
Fibre Channel: high speed network for data center storage networks
Firestop: restore a fire rated partition to it's fire rating after penetration with cabling.
Fishtape: semi-flexible rod used to retrieve cables or pull line.
FLAT: Flat Cable and Under-carpet cable
FMPR: Fiber Optic Multi Port Repeater

G

Ground loop: the flow of current caused by unequal ground potentials.
Ground: a connection between a circuit or equipment and the earth.

H

HC: Horizontal Cross-Connect
HDS: Horizontal Distribution System
HDSL: High Bit Rate Digital Subscriber Line
Headend: the main distribution point in a CATV system.
HFC: Hybrid fiber coax CATV network.
HIPPI: High Performance Parallel Interface, replaced by Fibre Channel
Horizontal crossconnect: connection of horizontal wiring to other equipment or cabling.
Horizontal: cable that runs from a work area outlet to the communications closet (Cabling Subsystem 3 in new TIA 568 nomenclature).
Host: large computer used with terminals, usually a mainframe.
Hub: a switch used to connect computers in a star network.
HYBRID: Mixed Media Conductor cables. In fiber optics, refers to cable with both singlemode and multimode fibers.
Hz: Frequency, Cycles per second.

I

IBDN: Integrated Building Distribution Network. NT Cabling System, Now owned by CDT for today.
IC: Intermediate Cross-connect
ICEA: Insulated Cable Engineers Association
ICEC: Insulated Cable Engineering Association
ICS: The IBM Cabling System
IDC: Insulation displacement connection, connecting wires by inserting or crimping cable into metal contacts that cut through the insulation, making contact with the wires.
IDC: Insulation Displacement Connector
IDF: Intermediate Distribution Frame
IEC: International Electrotechnical Committee, oversees international

communications standards.

IEEE: Institute of Electrical and Electronics Engineers, professional society that oversees network standards.

Impedance matching devices: a type of balun that matches impedance between two cables.

Impedance: the AC resistance.

Internet: a worldwide network of computers that allows communications between computers.

IRL: Inter Repeater Link

ISDN: Integrated Services Digital Network

ISO: International Standards Organization, oversees international standards.

IXC, Intermediate cross connect: connection point in the backbone cable between the main cross connect and the telecommunications closet.

J

Jacket: the outer protective covering of a cable.

J-hook: a hook shaped like the letter "J" used to suspend cables.

Jumper cable: A short cable with connectors on both ends used for interconnecting other cables or testing.

K

km: kilometer

Krone: Krone proprietary Cross Connect System

L

LAN: local area network, a group of computers and peripherals set up to communicate with each other.

LC: Small fiber optic connector with 1.25 mm ferrule.

Local loop: the interconnection of telephone central offices in a small region.

Loop resistance: measurement of the resistance of both wires in a pair measured from one end with the other end shorted.

Loss budget: The amount of power lost in the link. Often used in terms of the maximum amount of loss that can be tolerated by a given link.

M

MAC: Media Access Control

Main cross connect: the connection point between building entrance, backbone and equipment cables (Connection Point A in new TIA nomenclature).

Mainfame: large computer used to store and process massive amounts of data.

MAN: Metropolitan Area Network

Margin: The additional amount of loss that can be tolerated in a link.

MAU : Media Attachment Unit

MB/S: Mega Bits Per Second
MC: Main Cross-Connect
MDF: Main Distribution Frame
Mesh grip (aka Kellums grip): a grip made of wire mesh that grips the jacket of a cable for pulling.
Messenger cable: the aerial cable used to attach communications cable that has no strength member of its own.
MHz: Megahertz.
Modal dispersion: The temporal spreading of a pulse in an optical waveguide caused by modal effects.
MODEM: Modulator / Demodulator, typically a converter from one media/ protocol to another.
Modular 8: the proper name for the 8 pin connector used in EIA/TIA 568 standard, commonly called the RJ-45.
Modular jack: a female connector for wall or panel installation, mates with modular plugs.
Modular plug: a standard connector used with wire, with 4 to 10 contacts, to mate cables with modular jacks.
MP: Multi Purpose Cables
MSAU: Multi-Station Access Unit

N
N Series Conn.: Threaded Thicknet CXC Connector.
NA: Numerical Aperture, a measure of the angular acceptance of an optical fiber.
NCTA: National Cable TV Association
NEC: National Electrical Code, written by NFPA, sets standards for fire protection for construction.
NECA: National Electrical Contractors Association
NEMA: National Electrical Manufacturers Associations
Network interface (NI): the demarcation point where the public network connects to a private (commercial or residential) network.
Network: A system of cables, hardware and equipment used for communications.
NEXT: Near End Crosstalk, measure of interference between pairs in UTP cable.
NFPA: National Fire Protection Association, which writes the NEC in the USA.
NIC: Network Interface Card, used to interface computers to networks.
NII: National Information Infrastructure
NIST: National Institute of Standards and Technology, establishes primary standards in the USA.
NMS: Network Management System
NOS: Network Operating System: the software that allows computers on a network to share data and program files.

NVP, Nominal velocity of propagation : speed of an electrical signal in a cable, expressed relative to the speed of light.
NVP: Nominal Velocity of Propagation

O
OFN: Optical fiber non-conductive cable.
OFC: Optical fiber conductive cable.
OFNG or OFCG: optical fiber general purpose cable.
OFNR or OFCR: optical fiber riser rated cable for runs between floors.
OFNP or OFCP: optical fiber plenum-rated cable for use in air handling areas (plenums).
OFN-LS: Low smoke density optical fiber cable.
Ohm: Standard unit of electrical resistance.
OPM: Optical Power Meter
OSHA: Occupational Safety & Health Administration
OSI: Open Systems Interconnect

P
Passive optical LAN (POL): Premises network using passive optical network FTTH technology.
Patch panel: a cross-connection using jacks and patchcords to interconnect cables.
PBX or PABX: Private Branch Exchange or Private Automatic branch Exchange.
PCC: Premises Communications Cable
PCM: Pulse Coded Modulation
PIC: Plastic Insulated Conductor
Pigtail: A short length of fiber attached to a fiber optic component such as a laser or coupler.
PIN: PIN Photo Diode
Plenum: the air carrying portion of a heating or air conditioning system that can be used for running communications cables. Also a type of cable used in plenums, specially rated by the NEC.
POTS: plain old telephone service.
Power over Ethernet: Using data cables to provide power for connected devices. IEEE 802.3af or IEEE 802.3at.
Power Sum NEXT: Near end crosstalk tested with all pairs but one energized to find the total amount of crosstalk caused by simultaneous use of all pairs for communication.
Pulse dialing: old style phone dialing that works by making and breaking the current loop a number of times to indicate the number dialled.
Punch down tool: tool used to connect wire to IDC connections in punch down blocks.
Punch-down block: a connection block incorporating insulation displacement

connections for interconnecting copper wires with a special insertion tool.
   110 block: Punchdown block from AT&T 110 Cross Connect System.
   66 block: Punchdown block from AT&T 66 Cross Connect System.
   BIX: Northern Telecom proprietary In-building Cross Connect System.
   Krone: Krone proprietary Cross Connect System.
PVC: Polyvinyl Chloride

Q
QUAD: Four Conductor Cable.

R
Repeater, regenerator: A device that receives a signal and regenerates it for retransmission, used in long links.
Return loss: reflection from an impedance mismatch in a copper cable.
Reversed pair: a pair of wires in a UTP cable that have the two wires cross-connected in error.
RFI: Radio Frequency Interference
Ring (as in "TIP and RING"): one conductor in a phone line, connected to the "Ring" of the contact on old-fashioned phone plugs.
Ring: a network where computers are connected in series to form a ring. Each computer in turn has an opportunity to use the network.
RJ11: 6 Position Modular Jack/Plug used for POTS phones.
RJ-45: a modular 8 pin connector terminated in a USOC pin configuration, referring to a specific telephone application, but usually referring to the connector used in EIA/TIA 568 standard.

S
SC: Fiber optic connector with 2.5 mm ferrule in plastic snap-in body.
ScTP: screened twisted pair cable, UTP cable with a outer shield under the jacket to prevent interference.
Server: the center of a network where programs and data are stored.
Shorted pair: a pair of wires in a UTP cable that are electrically connected in error.
SNR: Signal To Noise Ratio
Split pair: a pair of wires in a UTP cable that have the two wires of two different pairs cross-connected in error.
SRL: Structural Return Loss, reflections in a copper cable caused by defects.
Star: a network where all the computers are connected to a central hub or server.
ST: Bayonet mount fiber optic connector with 2.5 mm ferrule.
STP: shielded twisted pair cable, where each pair has a metallic shield to prevent interference.
Structured cabling: a method of installing cable per industry standards to allow interoperability among vendors and upgrades.

Subscriber loop: connection of the end-user to the local central office telephone switch.

T

T568A: 4 pr. EIA/TIA Modular Plug Wiring Scheme ISDN.

T568B: 4 pr. EIA/TIA Modular Plug Wiring Scheme, AT&T.

Take off: reading drawings of a layout to get cable plant layout.

TC: Telecommunications Closet

TDM: Time Division Multiplexing

TDR: Time Domain Reflectometer

Telecommunications room (formerly closet): location inside a building for interconnection of backbone and horizontal cables (Connection Point C in new TIA nomenclature).

Telegraph: earliest form of long-distance communications, using coded letters.

Termination: Preparation of the end of a cable, e.g. optical fiber, to allow connection to another cable or an active device, sometimes also called "connectorization".

TIA: Telecommunications Industries Association

Time domain reflectometer (TDR): a testing device used for copper cable that operates like radar to find length, shorts or opens, and impedance mismatches.

Tip: one conductor in a phone line, connected to the "Tip" of the old-fashioned phone plug.

TO: Telecommunications Outlet / Connector

TOC: Telecommunications Outlet Connector

Token Ring: a ring architecture LAN developed by IBM. 4 MB/s and 16 MB/s versions are used.

Topology: the architecture or layout of a network, eg. bus, ring, star.

TP: Transition Point

TSB: TIA Technical Service Bulletin

U

USOC: Uniform Service Order Code, a UTP wiring scheme that allows 6 pin plugs to be used in 8 pin jacks for telephone use.

UTP: unshielded twisted pair cable, comprised of four pairs of conductors carefully manufacturer to preserve frequency characteristics.

V

Verification Tester: Tests cable plant using network signals.

Visual fault locator: A device that couples visible light into the fiber to allow visual tracing and testing of continuity. Some are bright enough to allow finding breaks in fiber through the cable jacket.

W

WAN: Wide Area Network

Watts: A linear measure of optical power, usually expressed in milliwatts (mW), microwatts (*W) or nanowatts (nW).

WiFi: Wireless data system, IEEE 802.11.

WiMAX : Wireless network technology, IEEE 802.16.

Wire mapping: confirming the proper connections of all four pairs.

Wireless: sending communications over radio waves.

Work area outlet: the outlet at the end of the horizontal cabling where equipment is connected with a patchcord (Connection Point D in new TIA nomenclature).

Work area: the location of the equipment connected to horizontal cabling. Sometimes called the telecom outlet (TO) or desktop.

Working margin: The difference (in dB) between the power budget and the loss budget (i.e. the excess power margin).

Z

Z, Zo: Impedance Symbol

ZSW: "Z" Station Wire or Quad Cable (same as QUAD).

Changes in TIA 568 Nomenclature in Revisions C and D(proposed)

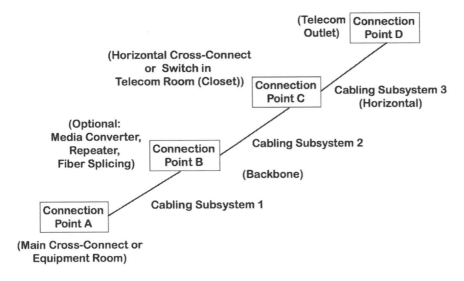

Appendix E
Additional References For Training and Study
For FOA Certification or Additional Knowledge

As with any fast-moving technology, keeping abreast of the latest technology, techniques and products can be a daunting task.

The FOA website, www.thefoa.org, has many pages of information on cabling and fiber optics. It has an Online Reference Guide, www.foaguide.org, with hundreds of pages of technical information and study guides for those preparing for FOA Certifications as well as for those interested in refreshing or increasing their knowledge of fiber optics.

The FOA has over 80 YouTube Videos including many lectures on fiber optics and premises cabling and demonstrations of hands-on installation. The FOA YouTube channel is "thefoainc" and links to the videos are on the Table of Contents of the FOA Online Reference Guide.

Fiber University, www.fiberu.org, is an online training center that has free tutorials and self-study programs using online and printed materials.

The FOA Reference Guide to Fiber Optics, Jim Hayes, is a comprehensive textbook on fiber optics used as the reference for FOA CFOT certification.

The FOA Reference Guide to Outside Plant Fiber Optics, Jim Hayes, is a comprehensive textbook on OSP fiber optics used as the reference for FOA CFOS/O certification.

FOA/NECA 301 Fiber Optic Installation Standard available from NECA (necanet.org) covers guidelines for fiber optic installation concisely. (Being revised in 2014)

Training Curriculum For Instructors
The FOA offers complete curriculum packages to simplify teaching fiber optic courses from this book. The curriculum packages include instructor guides, student manuals, PowerPoint slides, etc. Subjects available include basic fiber optics, advanced fiber optics and premises cabling. Details are available on the FOA website or by contacting the FOA.

Index
Finding Things In This Book

This book is adopting a lot of new ideas in creating a more useful book for reference and training, so we thought we'd try a new approach to the index also. Often when trying to find something in an index, you end up looking at dozens of pages before you find what you want.

We're going to try another approach, closer to a detailed Table of Contents with comments, organized by topics we think will be most likely sought. Start with the area of interest, then look for the subjects below. Let us know what you think.

The FOA Online Reference Guide has a Google Custom Search function that can help find specific topics or terms on the FOA site.

Chapter 2
Cabling Jargon 19

If you are looking for a definition of a term used in Premises Cabling, start here. If you are looking for a specific definition of a technical word, there is a Glossary in the FOA Online Reference Guide.

Chapter 5
Fiber Optic Cabling **75**

Chapter 6
Wireless... 101

31180480R00106